FOUR CENTURIES OF TURCO-BRITISH RELATIONS

STUDIES IN DIPLOMATIC ECONOMIC AND CULTURAL AFFAIRS

FOUR CENTURIES OF TURCO-BRITISH RELATIONS

STUDIES IN DIPLOMATIC ECONOMIC AND CULTURAL AFFAIRS

Edited by
WILLIAM HALE
and
ALI İHSAN BAĞIŞ

THE EOTHEN PRESS

British Library C.I.P.

Four centuries of Turco-British relations: studies in diplomatic economic and cultural affairs.
1. Great Britain – Foreign relations – Turkey
2. Turkey – Foreign relations – Great Britain
I. Hale, William II. Bagis, Ali Ihsan
303.4′8241′0561 DA47.9.T9

Typeset by Computape (Pickering) Ltd, Pickering, North Yorkshire

ISBN: 0 906719 070

CONTENTS

THE CONTRIBUTORS

Dr. William Hale is Senior Lecturer in Politics at Durham University. His publications include *The Political and Economic Development of Modern Turkey* (1981, repr. 1984) as well as several articles on modern Turkish history and politics.

Dr. Susan Skilliter is Lecturer in Turkish at Cambridge University. She is author of *William Harborne and the Trade with Turkey, 1578–1582* (1977) besides numerous articles on Ottoman diplomacy in the sixteenth century. She has also carried out research on Ottoman costume and court life at the time.

Dr. Colin Heywood has taught at several U.S. universities and is now Lecturer in the history of the Near and Middle East at the School of Oriental and African Studies, University of London.

Dr. Ali İhsan Bağış is Associate Professor of Economic and Diplomatic History in the Department of Economics, Faculty of Administrative Sciences, Hacettepe University, Ankara. He has published several articles and his two recent books are *Britain and the Struggle for the Integrity of the Ottoman Empire* and, in Turkish, *The Non-Muslims' Role in the Commerical Life of the Ottoman Empire, 1750–1839*.

Professor Mübahat Kütükoğlu is Professor of Ottoman History at the Faculty of Letters, Department of History, the University of Istanbul. She has published many articles; her two books are on economic relations between the Ottoman Empire and Great Britain.

Professor Osman Okyar is Professor of Economics in the Department of Economics, University of Hacettepe, Ankara. He founded the Department in 1969 and has been its chairman until recently. A member of the Board of the Foreign Policy Institute, Ankara, he has written extensively in Turkish and foreign periodicals on Turkish applied economics, Turkish economic history and foreign policy.

Professor Ömer Kürkçüoğlu is Professor of Diplomatic History and Dean of the Faculty of Economic and Administrative Sciences, Middle East Technical University, Ankara. Previously a member of the Faculty of Political Sciences, University of Ankara, he has also taught and undertaken research at the Middle East Centre, St. Antony's College, Oxford. A specialist in twentieth-century Turkish and Middle Eastern diplomatic history, his main publications are *Turkey's Policy Towards The Arab Middle East, 1945–1970* (1972, in Turkish), *Anglo-Turkish Relations, 1919–1926* (1978, in Turkish), and *The Arab Independence Movement Against the Ottoman Empire, 1908–1981* (1982, in Turkish).

Dr. Geoffrey Lewis is a Fellow of the British Academy and of St. Antony's College and Senior Lecturer in Turkish at the University of Oxford. His publications include *Modern Turkey* (1974), *The Book of Dede Korkut* (1974) and *The Atatürk I Knew* (1981).

FIRST FOREWORD

Sir Peter Laurence

It was on 14 January 1583 that the first English Ambassador to the Ottoman Sultan, William Harborne, set sail from England to take up his appointment. Four hundred years later I was his sixty-eighth successor, although one Ambassador, Stratford Canning, later Lord Stratford de Redcliffe, held the appointment on three separate occasions and so far holds the record for length of ambassadorial stay. It did not seem right to let the fourth centenary of this auspicious event pass without some appropriate celebration. A seminar on Anglo-Turkish relations held on 14 January 1983 in Hacettepe University in Ankara was a central part of this celebration, and the purpose of this book is to publish the papers presented at it by four Turkish and four British scholars in collected form.

The seminar was preceded by a lecture (included in these studies) which was given the evening before, 13 January 1983, by Dr. Susan Skilliter of Cambridge University in the lecture hall of the Turkish Historical Association on William Harborne himself.

The idea of the seminar was conceived in the Embassy. Its realisation required the co-operation of a great many others, and it gives me great pleasure to record that this was enthusiastically given when we approached them. First, of course, comes Hacettepe University, in the person of its Rector, Professor Yüksel Bozer, and the Vice-Rector, Professor Ahsen Orhon. Without hesitation they offered the use of their excellent seminar room and placed their guest-house at the disposal of the visiting British participants. Professor Emel Doğramacı, Dean of the Faculty of Letters, gave her full support and shared the chairmanship of the seminar with Dr. Skilliter. Professor Ercüment Kuran, of the Department of History, with whom I was able to collaborate very closely, did all the hard work over the practical details and organised the Turkish participation.

Secondly, our thanks are due to the scholars on both sides who undertook the time and trouble to prepare papers, and some of whom came a long way to attend the seminar. On the Turkish side were Dr. Ali İhsan Bağış of Hacettepe University, who has done much work on British economic policy; Professor Mübahat Kütükoğlu of Hacettepe University; Professor Ömer Kürkcüoğlu of the Middle East Technical University, who has studied the recent history of Anglo-Turkish relations; and Professor Osman Okyar, whose father was a close friend of Atatürk and his special envoy and later Ambassador in London. On the British side we had contributions from Dr William Hale of the Department of Politics of the University of Durham; Dr. Geoffrey Lewis of the Oriental Institute of Oxford University; and Dr. Colin Heywood of the School of Oriental and African Studies of the University of London. We also enjoyed the active presence of Professor Clement Dodd from the University of Hull and Dr. Andrew Mango of the B.B.C. External Services.

Thirdly, we are grateful to the British Academy and the British Council who generously met between them the travel expenses of the British participants.

In a one-day seminar it is not possible to review four whole centuries of Turco-British relations. We had therefore to be selective and concentrate on a few short periods or on some specific aspect which could be illuminated. Since trade was the reason for William Harborne's appointment in the first place, and remained our principal interest for the next 150 years or so, we started the proceedings by looking at our commercial and economic relations. Just as, however, the political/strategic importance of our relationship increased and in the nineteenth century predominated, so we moved on to consider certain aspects of this relationship, concluding with two papers on the Republican period.

We found it particularly gratifying that our celebrations on 13 and 14 January had an academic and cultural theme, because this has been one of the most fruitful sides of Turco-British relations, particularly in recent years. Each nation has derived great benefit from the study of the rich culture, history and language of the other, and has valued the tradition of close academic co-operation between two countries.

Over the whole board Turco-British relations are as healthy today as they have ever been. Turks and Britons have acquired a good understanding of each other. Their interests in the world largely coincide. And on those points where from time to time they may not, we do try honestly to resolve our differences with respect for the other's point of view. I hope and believe that this seminar has made its modest contribution to mutual understanding.

SECOND FOREWORD

Professor Emel Doğramacı

When I learnt that a seminar was suggested by the British Embassy to commemorate the fourth centenary of Anglo-Turkish relations I thought it was a very worth-while idea. Sir Peter Laurence gave his full and enthusiastic support, which was invaluable not only for the success of the seminar but also for the publication of the papers.

For the holding of the seminar the Rector of Hacettepe University, Professor Yüksel Bozer and the Vice-Rector, Professor Ahsen Orhon, generously provided facilities at their University. Thanks are also due to Professor Ercüment Kuran, who devoted precious time to the difficult organisational task of bringing together all the participants. Dr. William Hale and Dr. Ali Ihsan Bağış edited the papers: their contribution is greatly appreciated.

It was a great pleasure to have Professor Clement Dodd's presence during the seminar; his assistance with the publication of the papers in the English edition is gratefully acknowledged. The Turkish edition is ready for publication and it is hoped that in the not too distant future it will be available to the Turkish public.

It is my belief that this publication will significantly contribute towards, and help further develop, existing economic, political and cultural relations between Great Britain and Turkey.

ACKNOWLEDGEMENTS

The principal editor of the English edition wishes to record his appreciation to the Hacettepe University, Ankara, and to H.M. Foreign and Commonwealth Office for their valued contributions to the costs of producing this book to commemorate four hundred years of Turco-British relations. Thanks are especially due to Professor Emel Doğramacı of the Hacettepe University who participated in chairing the seminar and has assisted in the subsequent process of publication in invaluable ways. It has also been a great pleasure to work with Dr. Ali İhsan Bağış, the principal editor of the Turkish edition of this book, to be published by Hacettepe University. An especial word of thanks is also due to Professor Clement Dodd who has made the arrangements for the publication of the English edition of these papers.

I

INTRODUCTION: THE HISTORICAL BACKGROUND

William Hale

Britain's diplomatic relations with Turkey began in January 1583, when her first Ambassador to the Ottoman Sultan Murad III, William Harborne, set sail for Istanbul. This collection of papers was prepared to celebrate the four hundredth anniversary of what was to prove a difficult but politically momentous journey. Though it cannot claim to offer a complete or detailed survey of the totality of Turco-British relations over such a long period, it is hoped that it will provide a sketch of some of the currents which have affected their course.

There was some political motivation for the English desire to strike up relations with the Ottoman Empire in the late sixteenth century. Protestant England was at this time locked in a struggle with Catholic Spain. Friendship with the Ottoman ruler could represent a counterpoise to the naval power of the Spanish King Philip II, the 'head of the idol-worshippers', as the English described him to the Sultan.[1] As Susan Skilliter explains in her opening contribution, one of William Harborne's major achievements at the Ottoman court was to help prevent the renewal of the Hispano-Ottoman armistice in 1587. A second reason for this initiative was the anxiety of English merchants to gain a share of the important trade between the Ottoman dominions and Western Europe. Such was the predominance of commercial interests in the early Anglo-Turkish connection that the payment of the

Ambassador in Istanbul was for many years the responsibility of the merchants of the Levant Company rather than that of the English government.[2] Again, in this field, Harborne was remarkably successful. Within a year of his arrival he had secured a preferential customs tariff for English merchants, under which they paid substantially lower duties than other foreign traders.

Commerce retained an important role in Turco-British relations for the succeeding two centuries, but it could be profoundly affected by political aspects of the relationship. Colin Heywood's paper explains the attempts made by the English Government to achieve a peace between the Ottoman and Austrian empires in the 1680s and 1690s, and illustrates the complexity of the relations between Britain and Turkey at this time. After a good many upsets, the English Ambassadors' mediation efforts were crowned with success by the signature of the Treaty of Karlowitz between the Austrians and Ottomans in 1699.

It was only at the end of the eighteenth century that external conditions combined to force Britain and the Ottoman Empire together in a closer political relationship. Two developments contributed to this result. One was the southward expansion of the Russian Empire, marked by the Russian acquisition of the Crimea in 1774 to 1783. The other was the growth of British interests in the Eastern Mediterranean occasioned by the British conquest of India in the eighteenth century. Had Russia gained control of the Straits of the Bosphorus and Dardanelles she could have threatened the shortest British route to India. British statesmen thus realised the importance of forming some sort of alliance with Turkey against Russia. Apart from this, Napoleon's invasion of Egypt in 1798 brought the two countries together in an anti-French alliance.

Ali İhsan Bagış's paper draws attention to the continued link between commerce and politics during this period. Between the beginning of the eighteenth century and the 1780s, trade between Britain and Turkey suffered a long period of decline. This was partly due to the strenuous commercial activities of

France, partly to the fact that such newly-developed colonies as India and the West Indies had begun to replace the Ottoman Empire as a source of some imported commodities on the British market, and partly to the restrictive practices of the Levant Company. On the other hand, the Napoleonic invasion of Egypt ruined French trade in the Levant and gave British traders an exceptional opportunity to expand their business. Equally, as Dr Bagış explains, the free trade doctrines which were gaining ground in Britain at this time led to the abolition of the Company in 1825, and the subsequent long-term growth of Anglo-Turkish trade. This was enhanced by the Anglo-Turkish Commercial Convention of 1838, which prohibited all monopolies and allowed British merchants to trade anywhere in the Empire.[3]

The common political interests of the two countries were again brought to the fore by the occupation of Syria by Mehmet Ali Pasha, Governor of Egypt, during 1831 and 1832. The resultant Treaty of Hünkâr İskelesi gave Russian warships the right of passage through the Straits, while denying the same right to other powers. These conditions stung the British into action. When the Sultan's army suffered further defeats at the hands of Mehmet Ali in 1839 the British Foreign Secretary, Lord Palmerston, induced the Austrian, Prussian and Russian Governments to sign a joint Convention of 1840 which bound the signatories to confine Mehmet Ali to North Africa. An Anglo-Austrian fleet blockaded Beirut and the Egyptian army returned to its homeland.

The threat which Mehmet Ali represented to British interests was that his defeat of the Sultan might enable Russia to gain control of the Turkish Straits. A war between Russia and the Ottoman Empire erupted in what is now Romania in the autumn of 1853 and the Turkish fleet was subsequently destroyed by the Russian Admiral Nahimof in the harbour of Sinop. The British and French Governments had already moved their warships to the Sea of Marmara and in March 1854 they joined the Turks in a war against Russia in the Crimea. When the war was ended by the Treaty of Paris of 1856, Russia was forbidden to maintain naval forces in the

Black Sea and the Russian threat to the Ottoman Empire was stilled for the following twenty years.[4]

The threat arose again in the 1870s, when rebellion broke out in the Sultan's Bulgarian provinces. During the consequent Russo-Turkish war of 1877/8 the Russian armies were at first checked for four months by Osman Pasha's defence of the fortress of Plevne. In the interval, a European coalition against the Russian advance arose. Russian forces appeared before Istanbul in January 1878, but were met by a British fleet anchored in the Sea of Marmara. Russia was faced with the prospect of a new war against an Anglo-Turkish coalition, and backed down. By the Treaty of Berlin of July 1878, Russian territorial gains were confined to Romania and Batum and the Ottoman Empire secured a further lease of life.

As it was, the alliance of 1878 represented the high-water mark of Anglo-Turkish collaboration in the nineteenth century. In 1882 British forces conquered Egypt, still nominally a province of the Ottoman Empire, and thus acquired an Eastern Mediterranean base which did not depend for its effectiveness on an alliance with the Sultan. The downward drift of Anglo-Turkish relations continued to its nadir of the First World War.

By 1918, Turkey and the Central Powers were defeated and Britain and her allies exhausted. The following years saw some momentous changes in Turkey as Mustafa Kemal, later Atatürk, rallied the Turks in national resistance to the partition plan which the Entente powers hoped to impose on their country. As Ömer Kürkçüoğlu relates, the war between Greece and the Turkish nationalists for control of Western Anatolia was indirectly a war between Britain and the Turks, since Lloyd George's Government in London supported the Greek claims in Asia Minor. Even at the height of the military campaign, however, Atatürk was anxious to keep the diplomatic options open – as, for instance, in 1922, when he sent his colleague Fethi Okyar to London, to discover whether the British might countenance a Greek withdrawal without further bloodshed. The story of Fethi Bey's mission to London is told in detail by his son, Osman Okyar. After a head-on confrontation between the British and Turks at Çanakkale in September 1922, Lloyd George backed down, and the way was cleared for a lasting peace between Turkey and the former Entente powers, in the shape of the Treaty of Lausanne of July 1923.

Between 1923 and his death in 1938, Atatürk's paramount objective was to achieve the physical reconstruction of his country and its cultural and political reorientation. During the five years following Lausanne almost all the institutions of the old Ottoman Empire were swept aside – the Sultanate and Caliphate, the Islamic law and educational system, and the Arabic alphabet. Islam was not suppressed as a code of personal or communal belief, but was to be strictly divorced from politics. Correspondingly, Atatürk was anxious to restore Turkey to a respected position in the European comity of nations, as a stable, non-revolutionary force in the international system. Obviously, this meant mending his fences with the British as well as the other Western European states. For their part, the British accepted their moral defeat of 1922 and eventually began to turn back to Turkey as a potential ally against rivals in the Near East. For three years the reconciliation was held up by an Anglo-Turkish dispute over the status of Mosul, which had been left unsettled by the Lausanne Treaty. Eventually, in June 1926, Turkey accepted the allotment of Mosul to Iraq (then under British mandate). Just over three years later, in October 1929, the successful visit of a British fleet to Turkey symbolised the end of the Anglo-Turkish confrontation of the 1920s. By 1934, when Fethi Okyar began his second mission to London (this time as Ambassador) Britain and Turkey were moving back from hostility to alliance.

The original basis of this new alliance was the joint apprehension of Britain and Turkey at Italian designs in the Eastern Mediterranean. It appears that Atatürk never took the Duce's flamboyant claims as seriously as some of his contemporaries in Western Europe, but the danger which Fascist Italy represented could not be ignored. The Turkish Government had attempted to meet the danger in 1936 when it had played a leading role in the creation of the Balkan Entente between Turkey, Yugoslavia, Greece and Romania. The ultimate outcome was the Tripartite Treaty which Turkey signed with Britain and France in 1939. Of the Treaty's provisions, the most important from the British viewpoint was the undertaking to aid Britain and France in the event of an act of aggression by a European power leading to a war in the Mediterranean in which Britain and France were involved.[5]

The 'war in the Mediterranean area' which the Tripartite Treaty had envisaged became a reality in the autumn of 1940 when Mussolini invaded Greece, and Britain and the Axis powers began their struggle for control of the North African seaboard. The Turks, however, decided to preserve their neutrality. Turkey's involvement in the First World War had produced tragic consequences, and there was an understandable reluctance to enter the second conflict. There was, moreover, a special factor affecting Turkey's position, which the Tripartite Treaty had foreseen. Protocol 2 of the Treaty exempted Turkey from her obligations to the Allies if their execution involved her in armed conflict with the USSR. That danger had come alive in 1939, with the signature of the Nazi-Soviet pact.

It was only after the Nazi attack on Soviet Russia in 1941 that Britain began to press Turkey to enter the war on the Allies' side. The Turkish reply was that their army and air force lacked the equipment to perform the tasks which the British were demanding of it. The Turks also seem to have foreseen the possibility that if they joined the war against Hitler then the Germans might occupy part of Turkey and, as Ömer Kürkçüoğlu puts it, 'they did not want to be occupied by Germany only to be "liberated" by the Soviet Union at the end of the war'. That Stalin had designs on Turkish territory became all too clear in 1945 when he demanded the cession of Kars and Ardahan, the establishment of joint Turco-Soviet defence arrangements at the straits, and the revision of the 1936 Montreux Convention governing access through the straits, in favour of the Soviet Union. In the post-war world, his offensive pushed Turkey into the western camp in the emerging Cold War conflict. This alignment was sealed by her admission to NATO, together with Greece, in 1952. Britain's relations with Turkey thus became part of the multilateral structure of the western alliance.

Turkey's membership of NATO has never been in serious doubt, but some other issues have led to unrealised ambitions and occasional political divergences between Britain and Turkey. NATO's success in holding off the Soviet threat to Western Europe encouraged Britain and the United States in the belief that the principle of the multilateral alliance could be applied in areas outside Europe. This aim seemed to have come to fruition in 1955 with the formation of the Baghdad Pact by Turkey, Iraq, Pakistan, Iran and Britain. That the Baghdad Pact failed in its original purpose was hardly the fault of Turkey. The Arab leaders whom the Pact was intended to attract had never felt the hostility of the Soviet Union, whose position as enemy was in their eyes occupied by Israel. Britain's standing in the Arab world was severely damaged by her involvement in the Middle East war of 1956, and his alignment with Britain helped to bring about the downfall of Nuri al-Saiyid, the only Arab leader committed to the Pact organisation. The Central Treaty Organisation (CENTO) which emerged from the ashes of the Baghdad Pact after Nuri's overthrow in 1958 remained in formal existence for another two decades, but it never achieved the unified command structure which distinguishes NATO, and finally collapsed with the demise of the Shah's regime in Iran. In the meantime, Turkey has carefully reconstructed her relations with the Arab states and is currently, for instance, one of the few countries to enjoy close commercial and diplomatic links with both Iraq and Iran.

On the Cyprus question, Greece, Turkey and Britain, as well as the Cypriots themselves, reached a consensus in 1959/60, on the basis of the Treaty of Guarantee and the Cyprus constitution of 1960. Since then, however, things have hardly gone smoothly. The British Government declined Turkish proposals for a joint intervention in 1974, leaving Turkey to go it alone. More recently, it has refused to recognise the 'Turkish Republic of Northern Cyprus' set up in November 1983. On the other hand, both sides appear to accept the fact that Britain is no longer in any position to affect the future of Cyprus more than marginally, and would not oppose any settlement which was accepted by both the Greek and Turkish Cypriots. One can only hope that some sort of mutual accommodation will eventually be achieved.

The evolution of economic relations between the two countries since the foundation of the Turkish Republic is outlined in a separate chapter by the editor. Britain inherited a dominating role in the Ottoman Empire's foreign trade but, due to a variety of technical factors, her share of the Republic's foreign commerce fell during the inter-war period. It revived, however, during the latter part of the Second World War and during the post-war reconstruction phase. In the meantime, Turkish exports of some important commodities (notably chromite) caused some friction in the wartime relations between Turkey and the Allies. By the 1950s, Turkey's economy was back on a growth path; in absolute terms, her trade with Britain has increased substantially since then. As a proportion of her total trade, however, it has continued to decline, as other markets and suppliers have enlarged their role in the world economy. There have also been some important changes in the structure of Anglo-Turkish trade, since Turkey is now an exporter of a growing range of industrial products, besides primary commodities.

Finally, Geoffrey Lewis is right to remind us that the relations between the two countries have not just turned on high level diplomacy or the intricacies of commercial conventions. Over the centuries, thousands of ordinary Britons and Turks have had to get along with one another and, on the whole, they have done so remarkably well. Both nations have suffered from some occasionally ludicrous misapprehensions about the other and neither are much given to overt displays of emotion but, in the last analysis, there is a fund of mutual respect and goodwill which has managed to overcome a mountain of vicissitudes. It has survived for four hundred years and there seems no good reason to assume that it will not last for another four centuries.

NOTES

1. Akdes N. Kurat, *Türk-İngiliz Münasebetlerinin Başlangıcı ve Gelişmesi* (Ankara, 1953) p. 120.
2. M. Epstein, *The Early History of the Levant Company* (London, 1908) pp. 77–8.
3. Charles Issawi, *An Economic History of the Middle East and North Africa* (London, 1982) p. 19.
4. J.T. Shotwell and F. Deak, *Turkey at the Straits* (New York, 1940) pp. 41–3.
5. For text, see ibid., pp. 168–71.

II

WILLIAM HARBORNE, THE FIRST ENGLISH AMBASSADOR 1583–1588

Susan Skilliter

On 14 January 1583, in terrible weather, the *Susan* of London, a tall ship belonging to the newly-chartered Turkey Company, put in to Cowes on the Isle of Wight and took on board William Harborne, commissioned as the first English ambassador to Turkey. In this paper my aim is to bring the man and his mission back to life after four centuries.

Our hero was the second son of William Harebrowne, gentleman, and his wife Joan Piers, and was born in Great Yarmouth, Norfolk, a port on the East coast of England, about 1542.[1] His grandfather, George, was a Shropshire man, for some time Recorder of Shrewsbury, and the family traced its ancestry back to Sir Anthony who had fought in the army of Edward III. His mother's cousin, John Piers, became Archbishop of York in 1589. William had two brothers, Thomas, born before him, and Piers, baptised in 1558; and three sisters. The family lived in Yarmouth, in a house on South Quay, amidst all the bustle and activity of a busy harbour; from this it is easy to understand his choice of the mansion at Fındıklı to be the first embassy. His father was an active citizen; his name appears again and again in the records of the town, as Common Councilman, Bailiff, in 1575 as a Burgess in Parliament, and in 1576 just failing to become Member of Parliament for Great Yarmouth. Of his son's early life little is known. Probably he attended the newly-founded Grammar School at Yarmouth, leaving at seventeen or so to go abroad. Writing in 1584 he claims that 'twenty-five years of foreign travel (since my first passing the seas) have brought untimely age upon me, especially for the term spent in this country' – i.e. Turkey. He had a commercial career, working for some time as a factor of the great London merchant Edward Osborne, but not on his first mission to Turkey, 1578–1581, when he was a government agent, and refers to Osborne as 'my late master'. As a merchant his affairs must have prospered, for his name stands with Edward Osborne, Richard Staper, Thomas Cordell and Anthony Jenkinson, the great ones of overseas trade, in the list of the principal members of the Spanish Company, incorporated by royal charter in 1577. He had spent several years in Spain, probably collecting information there also for the Government, and was fluent in Spanish. In Turkey he used Italian, the *lingua franca* of the Levant, as his medium of communication, even in official letters to other Englishmen;[2] but he had never visited Italy, as he insists in a letter written in Italian to the Venetian Bailo, after being accused of giving secrets of Italian harbour installations to the Turkish authorities.[3] He did not know Turkish, but Edward Barton, his secretary and, later, his successor, did.[4] Latin was the diplomatic language of the Western embassies in Turkey, and Harborne wrote in Latin and probably spoke it, too; his reports are full of classical quotations. It is likely that he spent some time in the Baltic countries, where there had been a flourishing English trade since the 1550s, for he used the land route via Poland on three of his four journeys to and from Turkey;[5] he had a brother-in-law living in Lvov, as he told Sokollu Mehemmed Paşa, and in 1580, during his first visit to Turkey, we find him in Pera directing a trading venture for the export of Cretan wines to the Baltic ports of Danzig, Memel and Königsberg, on ships chartered in London.[6]

He was, then, first and foremost, a merchant, and so he was considered in Istanbul, by the other resident Christian ambassadors, of Venice, France and the Holy Roman Empire. This disdain is illustrated in the report of April 1586 of the Venetian Bailo Lorenzo Bernardo, who tells how Harborne sent his secretary Barton to greet the newly-arrived French ambassador, Jacques Savary de Lancosme, with a Latin address of welcome, as follows: 'The secretary began, "My Master the Ambassador," when the French Ambassador broke in in a rage, saying "Ambassador! why he is a merchant, your master, Ambassador! I know only one Ambassador at the Porte, and that is myself; out of this at once, and tell your master that he had better mind his trade and not usurp titles like these, or I'll have him drummed out of the place." The secretary greatly disturbed left, without a word; and when he reported to his Ambassador, the latter exclaimed, "I think that he won't be quite strong enough to turn me out." '[7] He had the qualities of a merchant, courage, intelligence, cunning and toughness; but he was also blunt, quick-temepered, ambitious and convivial, enjoying parties, when he was inclined to boast and divulge secrets. He had no claim to scholarship, as such, but he was well educated, and wrote copious reports in a rather pedantic style, with a very beautiful calligraphic hand. His memoranda on all subjects connected with the embassy and the Turkey trade, anonymous and many not previously attributed to him, are clear, detailed and, one feels, accurate and reliable; a hard-headed business man's view of the structure of the Ottoman court or the commercial value of the alliance to England. No scholar, but a writer, a linguist, and a traveller of enormous experience. He was an enthusiastic member of the reformed Church of England, taking the first embassy chaplain out with him in 1583.[8] It appears that he inclined towards Calvinism, if we may believe the Bailo Morosini who, in 1585, said of him: 'Everyone, for a joke, calls him Lutheran – even the very Pashas – much to his disgust, as he is a most desperate Calvinist'. For the Turks, certainly, the newly-arriving English were 'Luterān' – an inclusive term covering all the Protestant groups who had rebelled against the Pope's authority and claim to lead the Christian community and, hence, against those Christian powers who supported his claim. With his successors far into the seventeenth century, Harborne was to be for the Turks 'Luterān elçisi', the Lutheran ambassador responsible, in the

Ottoman Empire, for the citizens of Protestant states not yet in treaty with the Sultan.[9]

As for his right to be called a diplomat, and the founder of British Oriental diplomacy moreover, he was apprenticed to his craft in the field, during the three years spent in Turkey as an agent under cover of trade, directed by the Elizabethan spymaster, the Principal Secretary Dr Thomas Wilson.[10] His mission was to obtain national trading privileges, thus cutting out the Venetian middlemen, to enable the import into England of the goods specified in a Turkey Company petition of 1582:

> unwrought and wrought silk, spices of all sorts, galls, cotton wool and cotton yarn, grosgrains, camlets watered and unwatered, rice and wormseed, soap, oils, all kinds of drugs for apothecaries, linen cloth made of cotton wool, carpets and quilts of silk, alum, currants, damask, raisins, indigo for dyers, goats skins, as also buffs, wax and wool, dates and aniseeds, hides and fells.

The goods to be exported to Turkey were: 'Kersies of all sorts and colours, cloths, the like dyed and dressed, cottons, tin in bars, conyskins, pewter.'[11] This short list almost conceals the fact that what the English were offering were armaments, fine Kersey cloth for Janissary uniforms, the precious tin, not mined in the Ottoman Empire and necessary for casting cannon, lead from the roofs of ecclesiastical buildings demolished during the Reformation, old bells and broken metal statuary.[12]

On 1 July 1578 William Harborne left London secretly, having no official status and carrying no letter from Queen Elizabeth I to Sultan Murad III. He was accompanied by a certain Joseph Clements, who had made the journey in 1575 in order to procure a Turkish safe conduct for them. Carrying with them a sample consignment of Kersey cloths, lead and tin, they crossed over to Hamburg and proceeded thence to Danzig and on to Lvov. They found the city full of excitement. The King of Poland, Stephen Báthory, was in residence, in order to sign a new peace treaty with the Sultan, brought by two Turkish ambassadors, the Chiauses Ahmed and Mustafa. Harborne must have made himself known to them for, we are told:

> apparelling himself, his guide, and his servant after the Turkish fashion (having first obtained the king of Poland his safe conduct to pass at Kamenets, the frontier town of his dominions next unto Turkey), by good means he obtained favour of one Ahmet Chiaus, the Turks ambassador then in Poland and ready to return to Constantinople, to be received into his company and caravan.

Probably this chance meeting with the two Turkish envoys was the greatest bit of luck in all Harborne's diplomatic life. The second ambassador, Mustafa, a Hungarian renegade, was one of the Imperial Latin translators and a much-travelled Ottoman official. It must have been during this journey, as they rode leisurely and comfortably along the way, conversing in Latin, that he and Harborne became close friends and collaborators. The caravan left Lvov on 4 September and, passing through Moldavia, Wallachia, Bulgaria and Rumania, calling on the Voivodes as they went, they reached Istanbul on 28 October, Harborne in Turkish costume to disguise him from French and Venetian rivals.[13]

With his offer of a supply of armaments, in the first winter of the long war with Persia, and with the help of his new friends, by 7 March 1579 Harborne had negotiated the issue of a command to Queen Elizabeth by the Sultan, who thus, unusually in Ottoman procedure, opened the Anglo-Turkish correspondence.[14] Following upon the Queen's letter of thanks to the Sultan, dated at Greenwich on 25 October 1579,[15] a wider and more specific grant was prepared and issued in May 1580, within a month or two of the delivery of the royal letter.[16] This charter of privileges for the English nation, the basis of the whole Anglo-Turkish relationship thereafter, until the abolition of the capitulations under the terms of the Treaty of Lausanne in 1923, was based, almost word for word, on the French capitulations of 1569, and gave the English equal rights with all the established Christian allies of the Sultan. On 4 March 1580 an Imperial letter was sent to the Queen, recommending an Ottoman merchant Ahmed. accompanied by a certain Niqula.[17] We may suppose that these merchants, the first Ottoman mission to England, would have been expected, like Harborne, to supply information to their Government, and that they had been sent off at once to bring back news about a country which was quite unknown. The second Ottoman envoy to England was the master-spy Gabriel Defrens who, again under cover of trade, in September 1580 carried the original of the privileges, since lost, to the Queen.[18]

It was a great triumph for Harborne. He spent another year in Turkey, planning the establishment of the future embassy, carrying on trade, arranging a pilgrimage to the Holy Land, perhaps hoping that he would be commissioned on the spot as the ambassador now expected eagerly by the Turkish authorities. Instead, after having committed a diplomatic blunder which had international repercussions, he was fortunate to be released from house-arrest and able to start the journey, on 7 July 1581, along the same route through Moldavia and up to Danzig, arriving in London towards the end of the year. His name does not figure among the members of the Turkey Company, chartered on 11 September 1581; if that omission was a deliberate punishment, then it seems to be the only one he suffered. As soon as he reached England his knowledge and experience were recognized as essential for the organisation of the embassy and the trade, and apparently his disgrace was discounted; it is said that the Queen herself defrayed the expenses of the journey, amounting to 1500 ducats.[19] Moreover, as the privileges could not be confirmed and the projects of the Turkey merchants could not be achieved without the presence of the Queen's representative in Istanbul, before the autumn of 1582 it was decided that an ambassador should be sent out forthwith and that Harborne would be the most suitable man to fill the office. Thereupon, on 25 September William Harebrowne, for such had been his name for the first forty years of his life, was granted by patent the surname Harborne, for himself and his posterity, and a modified version of his family's coat of arms. He used his father's two crests, and the apt motto, 'Du loyall secrett'.[20]

Then, on 20 November 1582, Queen Elizabeth I of England commissioned William Harborne to be the first English ambassador resident at the court of the Ottoman Sultan Murad III, with these words:

> Whereas the most renowned and most invincible Prince, Zuldan Murad Can, the most mighty governor of the kingdom of Turkie, and Monarch of the East Empire, hath entered into league and friendship with us (which we, for our part, as much as lieth in us, do purpose solemnly and inviolably to keep in all times to come), and whereas, for the better countenancing and authorising of the same, the foresaid renowned Emperor hath granted unto our subjects free liberty of traffic in all parts of his sacred Empire . . . Know ye, that we thinking well and having good confidence in the singular trustiness, obedience, wisdom and disposition of our wellbeloved servant William Harebrowne, one of the Esquires of our body, towards us and our service, do by these chief presents make, ordain, and constitute him our true and undoubted Orator, Messenger, Deputy and Agent, giving and granting unto him power and authority, in our name and for us, to confirm the foresaid league and friendship, to take into his hands and to ratify the grant of the privileges, and to command and enjoin, by the authority of our Majesty, all and singular our subjects, trading and dealing in any of the coasts and kingdoms of that Empire, that as long as they remain in traffic with his subjects, they be obedient to the prescription and order of the foresaid privileges . . . Promising assuredly, and in the word of a Prince, that whatsoever shall be done of our said Orator and Agent, in all or in any of the premisses, not repugnant and contrary to our laws, shall be accepted, ratified and confirmed by us . . . Given at our Castle of Windsor, the 20. day of November, in the year of Christ 1582, and of our reign the 24.

These sentences are taken from the English translation of the document's Latin text, both of which were published by Richard Hakluyt in 1589, in the first edition of *The Principall Navigations, Voyages, Traffiques and Discoveries of the English nation*,[21] in which the documents and reports concerning

Turkey, printed so soon after their issue, form the basis of any study of Harborne's embassy.

Upon receiving the commission and the royal letters to be delivered to the Sultan, the Viziers and the High Admiral, Kılıç Ali Paşa, Harborne began the preparations for the voyage. The English sailing ships always had to make the journey to the Levant during the months of winter, when the galleys of hostile Spain, Italy and Malta were not patrolling the seas. The heavy luggage and the present for the Sultan, to be offered in her Majesty's name but paid for by the Turkey Company, were loaded on to the *Susan* of London, a Turkey Company ship of 300 tons burden, carrying fifty men and thirty-four guns, her Captain John Gray and Master Richard Parsons. They sailed from Blackwall in the Port of London on 14 November 1582, six days before the commissioning. A diary of the voyage was kept, anonymously, by one of the passengers, and published by Hakluyt in his second edition of 1600.[22] Thus we know that, when the *Susan* sailed from Blackwall, Harborne was not yet ambassador and was not on board. This must have been in obedience to the advice of Sir Francis Walsingham who, in his 'A consideration of the trade into Turkey', written in 1578, had warned that it was to be expected that 'the Venetians and the French king, having their ambassadors at Constantinople, will seek by some indirect practise to discountenance such of her Majesty's subjects as shall trade thither', and that the English envoy must perform his journey in great secrecy, 'for that otherwise the Italians that are here will seek underhand that he may be disgraced at his arrival there, and therefore it shall be very well done to give out that in respect of the danger of the traffic her Majesty cannot be induced that her Subjects shall trade thither.'[23]

So, early in December 1582, Harborne and some of his suite must have ridden quietly out of London and taken the road to Southampton, where they boarded the ferry for the short passage over to Cowes on the Isle of Wight.[24] But the *Susan* was late for the rendezvous, as the narrator tells us:

> by occasion of contrary weather we spent two months before we could recover the Cowes in the Isle of Wight. Where the 14 of January following we took in the worshipful Master William Hareborne, her Majesties Ambassador to the Turk, and his company, and sailed thence to Yarmouth in the foresaid Isle of Wight. The 19 we put from Wight. . . . The 31 in the morning appeared the Island of Cabrera. The first of February we put into a port in Mallorca called Porto de Sant Pedro; where they would have evil intreated us for coming into the harbour: we thought we might have been as bold there as in other places of Christendom, but it proved far otherwise.[25]

Certainly, it was a strange place to visit, although the port was secluded enough, well known to corsairs. It is on the south coast of the island, between Cala Figuera and Puerto Colón. Only large atlases show it today, but Piri Reis knew it well and describes it thus: 'Mezkûr limanın tekrar poyraz tarafinda, Porto Petre dirler, zikrolan limana misal, Hûdayi bir hub liman vardır. Ol limanın ağzında, yani lodos tarafinda, bir burgus var ve liman içinde bir hub akar su vardır. Bu zikrolan limanda barçalara kabil yerdir'.[26]

Terrible troubles ensued as the *Susan* lay becalmed in Porto Pedro, and Harborne's embassy came to the very brink of ruin before it had even begun. 'In the mean time,' the story continues:

> came in a ship of Marseilles, the Master whereof did know our Ambassador very well, with whom our Ambassador had conference, and with his merchants also. They came from Algiers in Barbary, which is under the government of the Great Turk. They did present our Ambassador with an ape, wherefore he made very much of them, and had them often aboard. By them, I suppose, he was bewrayed of his purpose as touching his message.

So, once again, Harborne had relaxed, and revealed the secret of his mission on Spanish territory. Word reached the authorities of the island and five of the ship's company, who had gone to a town nearby to buy provisions, were put in prison, and one of them, the purser, taken to Palma for interrogation. Finally, the Governor of the island arrived at the harbour with a force of 500 men and several guns which were hidden among the trees, trained on the *Susan*. All was ready for a battle; Harborne and the captain had donned their armour and, we are told, 'Our whole noise of trumpets were sounding on the poop with drum and flute, and a minion of brass on the summer deck, with two or three other pieces, always by our gunners traversed mouth to mouth with theirs on land, still looking when they on land should shoot, for to answer them again'.

Somehow, by a miracle, harmony was restored; letters were exchanged between the Governor and Harborne, masquerading as the captain, within three hours the men were released from prison and brought to the ship and, on 11 February, 'we shot off half a dozen pieces, hoist our sails, and departed on our voyage'. By 17 March they had reached Chios, where Harborne was given a rapturous welcome and naval reception by the Bĕg, the Emin and the French consul, all old acquaintances. After a short stay, on 29 March 1583, the *Susan* was towed into Istanbul by three galleys and, as they passed the Sultan's palace, all the ship's ordinance, thirty-four guns, were discharged, and twenty-four when Harborne landed and was received by a group of about sixty men on horseback.[27] That, briefly, is what the Englishman on board tells us of Harborne's arrival; but Gianfrancesco Morosini, the Venetian Bailo, gives a vivid account, tinged with some asperity, of how the event was viewed by the Christian quarter on land: 'On Good Friday', he writes:

> the ship entered the port, towed by two galleys, at the hour when the Christians were celebrating the Divine Office in their churches, by singing melodies suitable to the Passion of the Cross. Suddenly, when the vessel was off Seraglio Point, a great noise of artillery was heard, accompanied by a continual music of trumpets and drums and other signs of rejoicing, to the great grief and pain of these poor Christians who are here, when they saw that on such a day, and at such an hour, people who called themselves Christians acted in a way so contrary to the usage of the Church, and to the dishonour of such a solemn function. People were so deeply shocked that when the Ambassador went

> from his ship to his house, he was escorted by no Christians, only by Turks, and as he passed through the streets of Pera not a Christian raised his hat. And even the Turks, in contempt, call him a Lutheran, and show that they are far from pleased to see him; all the more so as on that very day the Ambassador provided a sumptious feast of meats, to which hardly the Turks would come, as even they abhorred in a Christian such an insult to his religion. That evening, on board ship, they had fireworks, salvoes of artillery and music, with great uproar. But they nearly paid the penalty of their sin, for one of the rockets fell back into the ship, close to the powder magazine, and set the ship on fire, and it was only with great difficulty that the fire was mastered.[28]

Morosini tells us that it was the Cavuşbaşi and the Kapıcıbaşı, with their retinues, who met him as he landed, 'and accompanied him to the house which had been hired for his dwelling'. This was 'Rapamat, my mansion house by Pera, over against Constantinople', the address with which Harborne ends his embassy correspondence. The house had belonged to Arap Ahmat Paşa, Beglerbeg of Cyprus, murdered by his own troops in 1578. Harborne must have chosen it during his first visit. It was on the shore of the Bosphorus at Fındıklı, occupying the site where the Güzel Sanatlar Akademisi stands today. Harborne had estimated for it in his usual careful way, thus:

> Our Mansion House and 2 gardens in the same. — The yearly rent of the same 30 aspers every day, and at the years end 10 pikes of fine cloth. 6 aspers a day for the gardener his wages besides his diet; which sort of people very much subject to drink we would gladly be excused of, with some other careful and practical young man from England, to supply their place, with less expense and to more content. All amounteth to aspers 14,140.

Harborne's list of his household, twenty-three persons in all, is arranged according to rank, headed by himself and three other gentlemen, Master John Wroth, Henry Violet and John Pont, without wages. Then 12 persons; his secretary, Edward Barton, and Peter Sęfton, the minister, Elias Osborne, Thomas Wilkinson, Christopher Keale, William Smith and

John Bailey, probably all merchants; four galley-slaves, two of them, John Bond and John Irish, already released. and two more, John Beer and Hammond Pond, expected to be released soon; last of all, the cook's boy. 'The expense of these 12', writes Harborne, 'cannot be less that 280 ducats yearly, besides their liveries'. Three others, John Bate, a merchant already established in Galata, his boy Stanley and Master Wroth's servant will be supported independently. Finally, William Hills, the tailor, Thomas Thompson, the horse-keeper, Emmanuel Welline and Mighell, the cook, whose wages, all four, were agreed in England at seventy-six ducats. Attached to the embassy, and on the payroll, were Mustafa, Harborne's old comrade, now chief dragoman, and his *sipahi*, Jacomo de Merzo, chief Christian dragoman, and Jacomo de Anthonio, the under-dragoman, and four janissaries.[29]

His house in order, old friends and old enemies saluted, the time came for Harborne to present the letters and gifts he had brought from the Queen. On 19 April he met the Grand Vizier, Siyawuş Paşa, and the other Viziers in the Imperial Divan, and on 26 April he made the presentation to the High Admiral Kılıç Ali Paşa, on board his galley.[30] Finally, on 3 May he was received in audience by Murad III in the Arz Odası of Topkapı Sarayı. The anonymous chronicler, one of Harborne's suite, describes the gifts thus:

> At our Ambassador's entering they followed that bare his presents, to say, twelve fine broad cloths, 2 pieces of fine Holland, 10 pieces of plate double gilt, 1 case of candlesticks, 2 very great cans or pots, and one lesser, one basin and ewer, 2 Poppinjays of silver, one with two heads, they were to drink in, 2 bottles with chains, 3 fair mastiffs in coats of red cloth, 3 spaniels, 2 bloodhounds, 1 common hunting hound, 2 greyhounds, 2 little dogs in coats of silk, 1 clock valued at 500 pounds sterling: over it was a forest with trees of silver, among the which were deers chased with dogs, and men on horseback following, men drawing of water, others carrying mine ore on barrows; on the top of the clock stood a castle, and on the castle a mill. All these were of silver, and the clock was round beset with jewels.[31]

After Harborne had been led forward and kissed the sleeve of the Sultan's coat, as the presents were being displayed, one by one, before the Sultan, he read out the Queen's letter of commendation and his oration in Latin, translated into Turkish, clause by clause by Mustafa, orally, the manuscripts being handed over afterwards to the Grand Vizier. Harborne's oration is in three parts. In the first part, addressing 'the most august and benign Caesar', he begins by praising the friendship into which the Queen has been invited by the Sultan. He conveys the greetings of the Queen, who is the most powerful and richest of all the Christian princes, as well as the unconquered defender of the true faith against all the idolaters falsely professing the Name of Christ. The Sultan should esteem her as the dearest above all his other allies, and friendship with her as the highest glory bestowed by Almighty God upon the Ottoman dynasty, welcoming Harborne as ambassador, with the great favour and honour befitting such a friendship. He has two petitions to make: first, that the customs should be alleviated on the goods which are brought on the long and dangerous journey from England, and are now cheaper through the cutting out of middlemen; and secondly, that an Englishman named Edward Bughens should be released from captivity in the Sultan's galleys.[32]

The second part of the oration is entitled 'A description of England presented to the Grand Signor'. That is what the Sultan heard, word for word, but translated now into English:

> England comprises 1,200 leagues in circumference; it has a great many splendid cities, of which the capital London is the same size as Istanbul; this has always 200,000 armed men in readiness. Within the country are 416 fortified towns, apart from castles, county-towns, villages, and country-houses scattered about everywhere. The land is very flat and exceptionally fertile, nowhere unproductive, most rich in fruits, cattle such as excellent horses and, above all, sheep, (for no wolves attack), whose wool almost equals fine linen in quality, honey, meat, fish, salt, wax, hides; moreover, its mines produce gold, silver, copper, tin, lead, bronze, iron, steel, saltpetre. It abounds in wood, both for constructing ships as for the fire, and sustains infinite craftsmen of

every kind. Neighbouring it there is another island called Ireland, of the same size, extremely fruitful but, because the islanders are unskilled, not so well cultivated. These two greatest islands of the world, with many other smaller ones, are subject to the rule of Elizabeth, the virgin Queen. From them, when need arises, 830,000 fighting men can be levied with great ease, men from 20 to 50 years, not counting those whose age is less or more, a fleet of ships and galleys larger and better equipped than those of all other Christian princes, so that their strength and power can hardly be described, unless seen. The people are quick and ferocious in avenging wrongs, most scrupulous in observing leagues and peace-treaties, and renewing them very generously on behalf of the hereditary monarchy, full of justice, extremely devoted to arms and the liberal arts, worshipping the Most Good and Most Great God in truth and humility, far from idolatry, hostile to, even loathing, those who profess the Name of God falsely.[33]

The third part turns from geography to history, recounting 'the estate and government of the most redoubted prince King Henry VIII and of his most royal progeny, with change of religion'. Here Harborne boosted the image of Queen Elizabeth and the role of the established religion, as well as beginning his campaign at the Ottoman court against Philip II of Spain.[34] Consequently, perhaps the most important achievement of his embassy was the bringing about of the cancellation of the renewal of the Hispano-Ottoman armistice by land and sea in 1587, since the insecurity thus created on Spain's Mediterranean flank may have helped to prevent the sending of the Armada against England that year.[35] The two petitions were also answered favourably; within a year the English had been granted a preferential customs tariff of 3 per cent, 2 per cent less than the 5 per cent paid by other foreigners, and at Harborne's departure in 1588 he could claim that he had had fifty-four Englishmen released and that none remained in captivity in the Ottoman Empire.[36]

During his five and a half years of residence Harborne founded the embassy firmly and promoted the trade, implementing the privileges by establishing consuls in Egypt, Syria, Algiers, Chios and Patras. Richard Hakluyt, in the dedication of his first edition of 1589 addressed to Sir Francis Walsingham, extols this great new achievement, asking: 'Who ever saw before this reign, an English ambassador in the stately porch of the Grand Signor at Constantinople? Who ever found English consuls and agents at Tripoli in Syria, at Aleppo, at Babylon, at Basra?' Nobody had ever seen or found such things before! William Harborne had proved, indeed, to be a trusty, obedient, wise and well-beloved servant of the Queen.

NOTES

1. For Harborne's early life see S.A. Skilliter, *William Harborne and the Trade with Turkey, 1578–1582* (Oxford, 1977) pp. 34–6.
2. See, for example, his letter of dismissal to the Consul of Chios, Thomas Osborne, 18 May 1585, published in Skilliter, 'Una vicenda d'intoleranza religiosa nella Chio Ottomana; il matrimonio del Console Osborne', *Il Veltro*, anno XXIII (1979) p. 332.
3. Harborne to Giovanni Moro, 20 April 1588; *Calendar of State Papers, Venice*, VIII, pp. 351–2.
4. His skill is attested by the historian Selānīkī; see the quotation from the unpublished part of his history in A. Refik Altınay, *Türkler ve Kraliçe Elizabet* (Istanbul, 1932) p. 12.
5. On this see Skilliter, *William Harborne*, pp. 39–46.
6. Ibid., pp. 110–15.
7. See *Cal. S.P. Ven.* VIII, p. 154.
8. This was Peter Sefton, minister; for the members of Harborne's staff see Skilliter, 'The Organization of the First English Embassy in Istanbul in 1583', *Asian Affairs* X (1979) pp. 159–65.
9. On the political importance of Protestantism for the early embassy see Skilliter, *William Harborne*, pp. 36–8.
10. For him see *Dictionary of National Biography LXII* at Wilson, Thomas (1525?–1581).
11. The petition is published in Skilliter, *William Harborne*, pp. 183–6.
12. For the trade in armaments see ibid., pp. 23–6.
13. The circumstances of the first journey are recorded by R. Hakluyt, *The Principal Navigations* V (ed. MacLehose, Glasgow, 1904) pp. 167–9; see also Skilliter, *William Harborne*, pp. 39–47.
14. For the Registry copy see ibid., pp. 49–50.
15. For this see ibid., pp. 69–72.
16. On the first English capitulations see ibid., pp. 86–103.
17. See ibid., pp. 77–8.
18. For him see Skilliter, 'The Sultan's Messenger, Gabriel Defrens: an

Ottoman master-spy of the sixteenth century', *Wiener Zeits. f. d. Kunde d. Morgenlandes* LXVIII (1976) pp. 47–59.

19. The details of Harborne's last year as an agent in Turkey, and his journey home, may be found in Skilliter, *William Harborne*, pp. 105–200.
20. See ibid., pp. 34–5.
21. See 1589 ed., pp. 176–7; McLehose ed. V, pp. 221–4.
22. See *The Voyage of the Susan of London to Constantinople*, in Hakluyt, *Navigations* V, pp. 243–58.
23. For this see Skilliter, *William Harborne*, pp. 27–32.
24. The Spanish Ambassador, Bernardino de Mendoza, reported to Philip II on 13 December 1582 that Harborne had left London, in disguise; *Cal. S.P. Spanish, 1580–1586*, p. 425: no. 301.
25. See *The Voyage of the Susan*, Hakluyt, V, pp. 243–4.
26. Transliterated from the facsimile edition, Piri Reis, *Kitabı Bahriye* (Istanbul, 1935) p. 536, lines 11–15.
27. See *The Voyage of the Susan*, Hakluyt, V, pp. 244–51.
28. From Morosini's report of 19 April 1583, *Cal. S.P. Ven.* VIII, pp. 52–3.
29. For this see Skilliter, 'The Organization of the First English Embassy', pp. 159–65.
30. For details of these visits see *The Voyage of the Susan*, Hakluyt, V. pp. 251–4.
31. For the audience with the Sultan see ibid., pp. 254–8.
32. For Harborne's Latin see Oxford, Bodleian MS Tanner 79, f. 192.
33. Latin copy in BL, Cotton MS Titus B. vi, f. 128*r*.
34. This follows the second oration; MS Titus B. vi, f. 128.
35. See Skilliter, 'The Hispano-Ottoman Armistice of 1581,' in C.E. Bosworth, ed., *Iran and Islam* (Edinburgh, 1971) p. 504.
36. Harborne informs Walsingham of the granting of his two requests in his report of 15 January 1584; *Cal. S.P. Foreign* XVIII, p. 308. See also *William Harborn his seruice . . . in his tenn yeares forrayne travell*, in H.G. Rawlinson, 'The Embassy of William Harborne to Constantinople, 1583–8', *Trans Roy. Hist. Soc.* 4th ser. vol. 5 (1922) pp. 21–2.

III

ENGLISH DIPLOMATIC RELATIONS WITH TURKEY, 1689–1698

C. J. Heywood

When, at the end of the seventeenth century, the Ottoman courtier-historian Fındıklılı Mehmed *silahdar ağa*, composed the invaluable chronicle of dynastic and military affairs which bears his name, he found space under the rubric of the *hicrî* year 1104 (i.e. 1692–3) for what he clearly regarded as an event of some significance. Sandwiched between a circumstantial account of the routing of a band of rebels in the province of Basra, and the narration of a complicated series of political manoeuvres leading to the dismissal of the Grand Vizier Çalik Ali Paşa, he noted the arrival at the court of the Sultan Ahmed II of an unnamed ambassador. As Silahdar records it:

> In order to interpose in and put an end to the bloody conflict (*kanlı cengi*) between the Sublime State and the Roman Emperor by means of an offer of mediation, the ambassador appointed by the king of England and sent out by way of Vienna and Belgrade, arrived at Edirne on Tuesday 4 Cumada'l-ahır (1104, i.e. 31 January 1693).[1]

The ambassador's cavalcade, we are told, passed close to the Imperial Palace, from where, unseen in the Saraçhane kiosk, the Sultan watched it pass by, and crossed the Saraçhane bridge over the river Tunca into the town and to the suburb of Timurtaş. There, in a house on the estate of the former Grand Vizier Maktûl Kara Mustafa Paşa, the ambassador and his suite took up residence and began to draw the daily allowances (*tayınât*) prescribed by the state in way of hospitality.

I have quoted this passage at length not merely to give an indication of the stately measures of late seventeenth century Ottoman historical prose, but because Silahdar's description of what we may now identify as the arrival at Edirne in January 1693 of William, Lord Paget, as Ambassador from William III to the Ottoman court, conveniently brings together a number of themes which are central to any examination of Anglo-Turkish relations in the last decade of the seventeenth century and which it is the intention of this paper to explore. To look ahead, Paget was to remain at the Porte for nearly a decade, having finally achieved in the autumn and winter of 1698/9, and in co-operation with his Dutch colleague, the States General's Ambassador at the Porte Jacobus Colyer, a mediated successful conclusion to that *kanlı cenk*, the long and bitter conflict between the Ottomans and Austria and her allies in the *Sacra Liga* – Poland, Venice, and, later, Russia – which had sprung from the ill-considered political ambitions of Kara Mustafa Paşa and the failure of his grandiose schemes before the walls of Vienna in 1683.

To look back from the vantage-point of 1693, not as far as the siege of Vienna, but only to the political upheavals in the autumn of 1688 which brought William of Orange to the English throne, Paget's arrival at Edirne is also significant, not only because he had served from 1689 to mid-1692 as William III's envoy at the court of the Austrian Emperor Leopold I and was thus uniquely qualified in his knowledge of both the Hapsburg and Ottoman courts. During the same period of five years no fewer than seven individuals had attempted with greater or lesser right to exercise the function, if not the title, of English ambassador to the Porte. Three had been ambassadors by right. Of these one, Sir William Trumbull, had been appointed by James II and had adroitly managed the transition to the new regime, being recalled in the summer of 1691. His successor, Sir William Hussey, had died of the plague at Edirne in the summer of the same year; Hussey's successor,

William Harbord, died at Belgrade on the journey out, less than a year later. The other four contenders, all in the confused eighteen months between the death of Hussey and the arrival of Paget, were the English embassy secretary and *de facto* chargé d'affaires Thomas Coke; the Dutch diplomat Coenraad van Heemskerck; the Dutch ambassador at the Porte, Jacobus Colyer, and the Italian soldier of fortune, polymath and Austrian agent Luigi Ferdinando Marsigli. As the witty and astute English merchant Percival Whitcomb, long a resident at Istanbul, commented in a letter to Trumbull written early in 1692, when the potential for dispute between Harbord and Colyer was being much discussed, 'our king has more public ministers here, or those that pretend to be so, than all the other Christian princes besides, and they are of all degrees and sizes, like a nest of boxes'.

Within the short space of an article it is impossible to do more than sketch in the complicated course of Anglo-Turkish diplomatic relations during these years at the end of the seventeenth century. The active role came almost entirely from the English side, or perhaps I should say from the side of William III himself and his closest advisors – the Dutch statesman Anthonie van Heinsius; the king's favourite Willem van Bentinck, later Duke of Portland; and the king's special agents at European courts, particularly the Dutch diplomat Jacob Hop, whose activities at Vienna in 1688 prepared the ground for the recognition by the stiffly Catholic but anti-Stuart Hapsburg court of William of Orange as *de facto* joint sovereign in England. The English secretaries of state – Shrewsbury, Nottingham and the rest – acted solely as the transmitters of William's instructions to English diplomats in the field. The aim of William's *Ostpolitik* was a simple one, and had already become fully worked out before the Revolution in England. It was founded on the belief that prospects for military success of the allies against France depended to a greater or lesser degree on the freeing of a large number of the Emperor's troops, together with their commanders, from the war in Hungary against the Ottomans, and their transfer to the Rhine and the Palatinate.

From the Ottoman side, too, had come an initiative for ending the war on negotiated terms. The loss of Buda in 1686, and the severe Ottoman defeat at Mohacs in the following year, brought about a *coup d'état* in Istanbul, the deposition of Mehemmed IV and the raising to the throne of his brother Suleyman II in the autumn of 1687. Under the influence of a peace party within the civil bureaucracy it was decided to send a mission to Vienna, ostensibly to announce the accession of Suleyman II but in fact to negotiate the best terms for peace. This mission, headed by the *reisulkuttab* or head of the Ottoman chancery Zulfikar Efendi and the chief interpreter to the Imperial Divan, Alexander Mavrocordato, did not reach Belgrade until September 1688, a few days after its capture by the Emperor's troops, or Vienna until February 1689, when the first of an ultimately fruitless series of Austro-Ottoman meetings was held.

These developments had not gone unnoticed by the Dutch – or by the English – at the Porte. Jacobus Colyer, the Resident for the States General at the Porte, sent news of Zulfikar's mission to Vienna to William of Orange, just at the moment when France was about to invade the Palatinate and thus activate the League of Augsburg against her and when William was on the brink of the descent on England. On 20 September the Dutch States General acted on William's instructions by offering Dutch mediation to the Emperor in securing an Austro-Ottoman peace, and Jacob Hop, then at Berlin, was sent to Vienna to support the work. In October, shortly before William crossed to England, Hop was at The Hague; 4 of November found him in Vienna, by which time Mavrocordato, the second Ottoman envoy, was already in correspondence with J. J. Hamel Bruynincx, the States General's permanent Resident at the Austrian court. These negotiations came to nothing: Austrian intransigence and lack of flexibility on the Ottoman side, the former still hoping to push south from Belgrade into the Balkans; the latter now believing that with the Emperor engaged on the Rhine, there was a chance of regaining Belgrade and the lost province of Hungary – both reasonable assumptions at that point – meant that the war continued. By the spring of 1689, with negotiations for the Grand Alliance approaching a successful outcome, it had become clear that the Emperor had committed himself to fighting a war on two fronts. A year later, in the spring of 1690, when Paget finally arrived in Vienna, there had been little change, but a cyphered despatch from him to Nottingham, written on 14 March only three days after his arrival, may indicate the opening of active English involvement in the mediation both at Vienna and at the Porte:

> If His Majesty would be pleased to direct Sir William Trumbull to endeavour an accomodation between this Crown and the Porte, proposals for it would be well received, but his first letters must be sent carefully by an Express for the settling of a sure correspondence, and to agree of a cypher in order to the better doing the business with secrecy.

But nothing was done, and Paget did not like Vienna or the Austrian court:

> I am now in a place where ecclesiastical power is so extremely great that no person that is not of their opinions can be looked on with any common civility; and therefore you may suppose negotiations go on slowly and heavily while their Priests are continually buzzing in their ears passive obedience to Mother Church which forbids all converse and sincerity of dealing with heretics, though the benefit will prove to be theirs.

The arrival of a new envoy from the States General in June – Coenraad van Heemskerck, with whom Paget was to be embroiled for the next four years – brought about an Anglo-Dutch proposal for joint mediation if the Austrian court could be induced to state the terms on which it could be persuaded to negotiate with the Ottomans. It could not, and Ottoman successes in the campaign of 1690 – Belgrade was retaken in October, following the recapture by the Grand Vizier Mustafa Köprülü of Vidin, Nish and Smederovo – raised fears amongst the allies of a separate peace between the Emperor and France. The arrival in Vienna of Trumbull's successor at the Porte, Sir

William Hussey, in November 1690, did not materially alter the situation there. At the Porte, too, during this period, there had been much activity. Trumbull had arrived in Istanbul in August 1687. Already during the tenure of his predecessor, Chandos, the suggestion had been made that for the benefits which might accrue to English trade and commerce mediation should be offered between the Emperor and the Porte, but a Cabinet meeting in early 1687 rejected it. Attempts by Trumbull in 1688 to interest the Levant Company in Zulfikar's mission to Vienna came to nothing, the Company hastily backing away from any suggestion of English diplomatic initiatives. This lack of enthusiasm among the London merchants suited Trumbull: 'it is highly satisfactory to me', he wrote in reply, 'to be freed from the trouble and hazard of such a negotiation'.

The news of the Revolution in England was slow in reaching Istanbul. Finally, in March 1689 came news of the deposition and flight of James and the success of William of Orange: 'such a miraculous deliverence' Trumbull burst out to his correspondent Everard Fawkener, 'from the accursed Jesuiticall Popish designs against our religion and liberty', and immediately attempted to gain copies of letters which it was believed the States General had sent to the Porte, and to begin to establish a close relationship with the Dutch resident Colyer. Trumbull's heart, however, was not in it: he had already written opportunely to Shrewsbury that he 'had willingly entered this banishment for the sake of my Religion, as things stood then in England', but was now anxious to return home. The Levant Company, on the other hand, were bent on keeping Trumbull at the Porte to avoid the heavy expense of sending out a new ambassador, and Trumbull's old enemy and predecessor, Chandos, was showing signs of wanting to return to Turkey. 'Chandos', wrote Trumbull to his friend Sir Charles Cotterell, 'is so much my friend as to labour exceedingly to get me recalled, that he may return again to this blessed embassy, which God grant'. William, however, confirmed Trumbull for the time being, in August 1689; the news did not reach him for nearly a year.

Before that, in the late summer of 1689, Trumbull was actively engaged with Colyer, unofficially, in attempts at mediation. The campaign of 1689 had gone badly for the Ottomans: it had ended for them in defeat at the hands of Louis of Baden near Batochin on 30 August; seventeen days later, in a general council of war held at Sofia, it was decided to accept the Austrian terms, severe as they were, as long as the Emperor could be persuaded to give up Belgrade and accept Temesvar or some other place in lieu of it. The Poles could have Caminiec if they wanted, and Venice could keep its conquests in the Morea. This looked hopeful, but French money and Ottoman unwillingness to admit defeat prevailed: the Grand Vizier Bekri Mustafa Paşa was overthrown in late October, and Mustafa Köprülü raised to the Grand Vizierate. Trumbull and Colyer fell out, partly over the failure of the Dutch dragoman Theyles to achieve anything at Edirne; partly over Colyer's own refusal to forward Trumbull's despatches from Edirne. By New Year's Day 1690 Trumbull was stigmatising the Dutch resident as '[in] his dealing insincere and treacherous; [in] his correspondence useless and insipid.' Thus the first brief period of Anglo-Dutch co-operation at the Porte came to an end.

It would be time-consuming to continue this account of Anglo-Dutch relations at the Porte during these years in comparable detail, but the failure of Trumbull and Colyer to co-ordinate their policies was to be imitated in the next few years by their successors. The reasons are complex, although often they seem to have been little more than a clash of personalities. Much of the blame for the poor success of English diplomacy during the earlier part of William's reign must, however, be placed on what may be described as institutional causes. Chief among these was the separation for much of the time of the Ottoman court and of the ambassadors attached to it. After the overthrow of Mehemmed IV his successors, wary of the political power of the Istanbul mob, preferred to live at Edirne. Trumbull, at Istanbul, was ill-placed to open up any serious English negotiations with the Porte. The normal channel of communication between an ambassador and the Porte were the embassy dragomans, but these worthies were the responsibility of the Levant Company and not the Crown. In any case, Trumbull had a very dim view of the dragomans in his service: terms such as 'laziness', 'falseness' and 'incapacity' were bandied about in his despatches. To make matters worse, the English dragomanate was under strength: only two were currently employed instead of the three provided for by Company rules. The senior dragoman, Antonio Perone, was very aged and was troubled by deafness; the second dragoman, Timone ('Signor Dimetrasco') was considered to be unfit for promotion. There were also the so-called *giovanne di lingua*, or trainee interpreters, but three years of daily study with a *hoca* in Trumbull's own house had had no results, and Trumbull despaired of their ever gaining proficiency in the Turkish language.

Equal difficulties surrounded Trumbull in his attempt to make use of the permanent secretary to the embassy. This post, in the terminology of the time that of *cancellarius*, was held by a certain Thomas Coke, who had spent his entire working career in the Ottoman Empire and possessed an unequalled knowledge of Ottoman society. For reasons which remain obscure he was unwilling to place this knowledge at the disposal of new ambassadors (he had been stationed in Istanbul since at least 1668), and politically his views were somewhat radical, as witness a dinner-table conversation in 1680, reported by an earlier ambassador, Sir John Finch:

> Mr Coke had averred that if the king opposed the interest of the people he might by them be cut off, which I declaring to be treason, Mr Coke replied that Mr Hampden and several others were present when he spoke to Mr Whitcombe, and that he said that if the king would introduce Turcism or Paganism or Judaism or Popery, he would put the people to their thoughts. Upon this Mr Whitcomb replied that Mr Coke had several times declared the whole body of the people were above the king and that he (Coke) was a perfect Miltonian.

Trumbull and he got on very well, however, and later Paget stationed him at Edirne to act as unofficial agent; but his health gave way and he was to die late in 1694, still unreconstructed in his political opinions.

These personnel difficulties apart, which were compounded by the Levant Company's unwillingness to countenance any financial support for what it regarded as political matters, the chief problem facing Trumbull and his successors was the finding of a convenient, secure and reasonably rapid route for communication with London.

William III's concept of mediation diplomacy may indeed be regarded as distinctly modern, but the means of effecting it were less so, and the rigours of present day shuttle diplomacy may be measured to their disadvantage in the scale of their seventeenth-century equivalents. The chief problem was one of ensuring the rapid and secure transmission of despatches between London and the Porte. The long axis of William III's diplomacy joined London and The Hague with Vienna and Edirne or Istanbul, thus enforcing the use of land routes between London and the Porte, the sea route being either long and dangerous via the Straits of Gibraltar, or in any case closed to English traffic after the outbreak of war with France. As early as March 1689 the route from England to Turkey via Marseilles had become hazardous, and Trumbull was busy attempting to open up communications via Venice or Livorno. On 15 April Shrewsbury ordered all merchant ships to travel in convoy 'there being reason to expect a rupture between us and France', and as early as December 1688 the Levant Company in London had written to warn Trumbull of the imminence of 'a speedy break with France' and ordering him to write to the consuls at Aleppo and Izmir to advise 'all commanders of ships to be very cautious and not to trust the French nor any other nation unless it be the Dutch'. Thus, from the outbreak of the war, English shipping in the Mediterranean was much curtailed. The ships which did sail, sailed under convoy, with inevitably further delays, or even losses. Orders sent by the Levant Company to Trumbull on 13 December 1689 were not received by him until 25 October 1690 – by no means the worst example of untoward delays.

A classic example is provided by the fate of the instructions sent by William III to Trumbull in the summer of 1689. The news of the outbreak of war with France had been communicated by the Levant Company in a letter of 19 April, which appears to have been forwarded by the sea route, and to have reached Trumbull on 5 or 6 June in the good time of forty-eight or forty-nine days. On this very day, 6 June, William III caused to be drawn up new instructions for Trumbull, ordering him to attempt to mediate a peace between Austria and the Porte. These were sent out in charge of Paget, as far as Regensburg, from whence they can be traced to the English consul at Venice. We next catch sight of them in Zante in the Ionian Islands in April 1690, and at Izmir on or about 9 May. From Izmir they were sent overland to Istanbul and were delivered into Trumbull's hands on 4 June 1690, two days less than a year after they had left London.

Of course this was an exceptionally bad case, and one equalled only by further despatches and instructions from the Secretaries of State's Office and from the King himself, written in November and December 1689 and sent out by sea on the *Loyalty*, which struggled into Istanbul late in November 1690.

By the time Hussey reached the Porte, matters had somewhat improved. Instead of the roughly 120 to 180 days taken by most of the early despatches from London to Trumbull, Hussey in the summer of 1691 got two of his despatches from Istanbul to London in seventy-nine days via Dubrovnik and Venice and sixty-three days via Wallachia, respectively; while his last despatch from Edrine, written on 29 August 1691 only a few days before his death, and sent by special courier via Wallachia and Vienna, reached London on 17 October, only fifty-one days later. Two earlier despatches, sent from Istanbul on 29 July and 1 August, however, failed to arrive at their destination. The chance of delay or loss befalling a particular despatch could be reduced to a minimum by sending duplicates by different routes. John Evans, a Levant Company merchant, sent his letters to Paget in 1695 in no less than four copies by four different routes, for example, in May of that year, (a) direct from London to Istanbul by sea in the *Delaval* galley; (b) under cover to Paget's continental banker at Frankfurt, Isaac Behagel, to be forwarded by him; (c) under cover to the then English Ambassador at Vienna, Lexington; and (d) via the English consul at Livorno. As Paget had written two years earlier to the Secretary of State Nottingham, from Edirne:

> No regular posts pass in this Country, nor is there any direct way for conveyance of correspondence: . . . be pleased to direct your letters to the English consul at Leghorn, thence to be forwarded by the way of Smyrna; and a copy of the same by the way of Vienna, (and) one of the two will surely come to hand.

Later, in 1696, we find Paget communicating with Vienna via Herrmannstadt in Transylvania, and the commander of the Austrian forces there, Rabutin. Before this, almost from the time of his arrival at the Porte, Paget had employed the kahya of the hospodar of Wallachia Constantine Brancoveanu as an intermediary, and forwarded some of his despatches to Vienna and London by that route. As a result, the transmission times for Paget's despatches showed a steady reduction during the years 1692 to 1698. In the summers of 1695 and 1696 London and the Porte were on occasion only fifty-six days apart, and by January 1698 Paget at Edirne was able to get his despatches to London in 42 days by special courier, riding at an average of fifty miles a day. The courier in question was Paget's redoubtable secretary, G.P. Schreyer who, between late January and late June 1698, when the negotiations between the Porte, Vienna and London were at their most critical stage, was almost continually in the saddle, journeying from the Porte once to London and twice to Vienna. In September 1698, just before the opening of the Congress at Karlowitz, he was again despatched by Paget, this time from Belgrade to Vienna and return, and on 27 January 1699, the day after the signing of the treaty which ended the long seventeen years' war, he left

Karlowitz to carry the news of the settlement to London, returning to Edirne early in May. Thus, in the space of 16 months Schreyer covered on horseback at least 12,000 miles. (Schreyer died in Istanbul early in 1702: his tombstone, well preserved, may still be seen in the cemetery at Feriköy.)

In spite of these difficulties, and many others, and in spite of discouragements, the tenuous chain of William III's *Ostpolitik* remained unbroken. Ambassadors succeeded one another; Trumbull sailed for England and the post of Secretary of State in the summer of 1691; a few weeks later his successor Hussey, who had come out with high hopes, died of the plague at Edirne; and Hussey's successor, William Harbord died (as we have noticed) at Belgrade in the summer of 1692. Paget's arrival at the Porte in January 1693, with which we opened this paper, was followed by inconclusive negotiations with the Ottomans and by a monumental quarrel with his Vienna colleague van Heemskerck, who had preceded him to the Porte and who had in Paget's eyes compounded his impertinence in attempting to introduce the latter at the Ottoman court by making a series of ill-judged peace proposals which gave the Ottomans the perfect excuse for refusing Paget's own more judicious and balanced terms. After almost two years at Istanbul Paget had achieved nothing, and felt that nothing could be achieved until the military stalemate which had lasted since the campaign season of 1692 could be broken one way or the other. Much of 1695 Paget spent at Edirne, but again fruitlessly: the death of the Sultan Ahmed II and the accession of Mustafa II brought about a revival of Ottoman military fortunes in the campaigns of 1695 and 1696, and Anglo-Ottoman relations reached a low point in 1696, with a solidly pro-French regime under the Grand Vizier Elmas Mehmed Paşa and the English in disgrace for allegedly privateering in Ottoman waters. In June 1697 Paget went once more to Edirne with a list of grievances, not to negotiate, but returned empty-handed to Istanbul, hoping soon to return to England via Belgrade and Vienna, his successor having already been nominated.

At this point, unexpectedly, the tide turned. In the west the war between the allies and Louis XIV had been winding down, the implications of which Mustafa II and his advisors had totally ignored. As a result, on 12 September 1697, the day after the signing of the Treaty of Ryswyck, the Ottoman army intent on regaining Hungary and building on the successes of the two previous campaigns, was shattered in the battle of Zenta. The Grand Vizier was killed, the remnants of the army and the Ottoman high command fell back on Belgrade, where on the 18th the commander of the fortress, Amcazade Huseyn Paşa was appointed to the Grand Vizierate. The new Grand Vizier arrived in Edirne at the end of October, and a long series of *divan* meetings were held to determine Ottoman policy. Paget was now summoned to Edirne and at Edirne in December 1697 and January 1698 negotiated single-handed with Huseyn Paşa the bases of the future peace settlement. The English proposals of 1693 for a peace on the basis of each side keeping what territory it held at the conclusion of hostilities were reactivated and, after a tactical withdrawal of Ottoman claims to Transylvania, tacitly accepted by the *divan* on 10 January and by the *shaykhulislam*, the influential advisor of Mustafa II, Feyzullah Efendi, a few days later. The mediation of William III was accepted, and letters were written by the Grand Vizier to the King signifying as much. Schreyer, Paget's secretary, was sent off post-haste to London, and for the Ottomans the die was cast. The pacific and realistic policies of Huseyn Köprülü, directed towards a mediated peace, had been adopted; and for Paget, the mediation which he and his predecessors had striven for during nine years had been accepted. The putting into effect of the mediation, the lengthy negotiations in person and by correspondence between Paget and Mavrocordato on the one hand and the Austrian chancellor Kinsky on the other, which led to the opening of the peace Congress at Karlowitz in October 1698, and the course of the Congress itself, form a further chapter in the long history of Anglo-Turkish diplomatic relations.

NOTES

1. For bibliographical details, and references to the sources used for the production of this paper, see the author's (unpublished) London Ph.D. thesis, 'English Diplomacy between Austria and the Ottoman Empire in the War of the Sacra Liga, 1684–1699, with special reference to the period 1689–1699' (1970). A revised and expanded version of this work is in course of preparation.

IV

BRITISH ECONOMIC POLICY IN THE OTTOMAN EMPIRE UNDER GEORGE III

Ali İhsan Bağış

The relationship which began in the second half of the sixteenth century between Britain and the Ottoman Empire was a commercial one. Over the years, trade had its ups and downs. Its most flourishing period ran from 1620 until 1683. This flourishing trade entered into a period of decline[1] at the beginning of the eighteenth century.

At this time, trade with the Ottoman Empire was monopolised by the Levant Company, which had been established in 1581. No one could trade in the Ottoman dominions except the members of the Company, and it was not easy to be a member. Whenever occasion arose, the adversaries of the Company criticised and attacked it, since they attributed the decline of trade to the Company's monopolistic nature.

When George III came to the throne in 1760 the trade with the Ottoman Empire was at 'its lowest ebb'.[2] The British Ambassador complained bitterly in the eighteenth century about the deplorable state of the trade. Of course the causes of decline were discussed and studied, and it was usually attributed to the French, who were then successful in the Empire. This was only partly true however; during the second half of the eighteenth century, the British East India Company's success also had some impact on the Levant Company's trade. For example, the East India Company merchants established themselves in Basra and replaced Aleppo for the 'barter of English cloth and Persian silk'. In 1767 the Levant Company's trade fell so badly that the Company was compelled to apply to the Government for aid. In 1768, 1770 and in 1775 the Company received £5000 on each occasion from the Government to pay its debts. James Porter, the British Ambassador in 1768, was to observe that the British trade in the Levant 'had sunk to such a degree that the Channel remains almost without hope of replenishing'.[3]

Moreover, the Russo-Turkish war of 1768–1774 had produced 'a great stagnation' of trade; this greatly weakened the good relations hitherto existing between the Porte and the British Government. The fact was that Britain had given assistance to the Russian fleet, which in 1770 had sailed from the Baltic to the Mediterranean and which had, on 10 July 1770, burnt and destroyed the Ottoman fleet in the harbour of Çeşme. The Ottoman Government believed that the aid which Britain had granted to the Russians was responsible in no small degree for the disaster which befell the Ottomans at Çeşme. The attitude of the Porte therefore became rather cold and hostile towards Great Britain. Threats were indeed made against the factories of the Levant Company at Istanbul and Izmir and against British trade in general.[4]

After the Russo-Turkish war the Russians also began to enter into the Ottoman market. For a time they even took over the iron market from the English merchants. The Russians also replaced the Levant Company in the trade in furs, which British merchants brought from Canada.[5] On the other hand, before the French Revolution, France accounted for three-fifths of the total European trade with the Ottomans while the British had one fifth.[6] German and Venetian cloth as well as manufactured cotton goods also began to be exported via Trieste in large quantities to the Ottoman market. Lastly, during these crucial years, cotton was poured into England from the East Indies, at lower prices than that imported by the Levant Company.

The Government, however, was not willing to allow the trade to be ruined. Thus, when granting the sum of £5000 to the Levant Company in 1775,[7] George III instructed his newly appointed Ambassador to Istanbul, 'to act in the best and most influential manner and to be firm and active in maintaining all the privileges given to British trade'. Sir Robert Ainslie, the Ambassador, was also to do all in his power to give satisfaction to the Levant Company's merchants.[8] But the Ambassador was not sanguine about the situation and in 1779 informed London that 'trade had been totally interrupted and not a single English ship had reached Istanbul for eight months'.[9] Moreover, commerce was worsened by the American War of Independence in 1779, which 'reduced the trade to desperate straits'. To keep the Levant Company alive, the Government supported an Act in 1780 waiving the requirements of the navigation laws and permitting the imports of Levant Company goods in British or foreign ships from any port during the war. But the cotton growers of the British West Indies protested that the free import of cotton from any place within the Mediterranean would damage all who were interested in the trade to the West Indies. In spite of these steps it was still reported in 1781 that the 'business was in a most deplorable situation'.[10]

None the less, in 1784 Sir Robert Ainslie, the British Ambassador in Istanbul, as a result of his joint mediation with the French ambassador on the annexation of the Crimea by Russia,[11] was able to secure the privilege of exemption of the Masteria duty[12] from the Porte for British merchants.[13] The Masteria duty was a customs duty imposed on European commodities imported into the Ottoman Empire. But this limited success by itself was not enough to improve British commerce. Nor was the Ambassador optimistic regarding Black Sea trade, since the French and the others were very enthusiastic about the latter. As far as Sir Robert Ainslie was concerned, this recently-developed trade 'can produce little real advantage, but like the Lincolnshire proverb is only much cry and little wool'.[14] Yet the Ambassador did not discourage merchant called David Gray from travelling to explore the commercial possibilities in the Black Sea region and the Crimea. After his journey Gray prepared a report suggesting the Government help which was needed especially in the fields of timber and tobacco.[15] It seems that nothing came of this.

None the less, a few years later, with the idea of encouraging British sales to the Crimea and the Black Sea, a Levant Company merchant called Richard Willis published a book in London in 1787.[16] None of these made a serious impact on the Government. The fact was that with the exception of the Levant Company's merchants, the British were neither politically nor commercially concerned with the Ottoman Empire. At this time the affairs of the Empire had no special prominence in the eyes of the statesmen and politicians in London.

In 1784, however, a Government change took place in London and William Pitt the Younger became Prime Minister. Although Pitt was to become the adversary of the integrity of the Ottoman Empire in 1791, at this stage he was not concerned with it. For Pitt aimed above all at success in domestic affairs; the Irish problem, the national debt, finance and naval affairs occupied Pitt's mind more than the problem of foreign relations. During his first years in power Pitt was rather cautious and reserved towards continental involvement. Pitt was not advocating isolation; indeed he wished to emerge from it as soon as he could and searched for the means to do so, though very cautiously.[17] In 1786 Pitt concerned himself more with the Russian trade than the Levant, and was inclined to seek the renewal of the Anglo-Russian commercial treaty which was concluded in 1766 and due for renewal in 1786. However, Catherine II wanted Britain to acquiesce in her ambitions against the Ottoman Empire. Pitt, on the other hand, was very cautious and reserved towards political involvement and merely talked in terms of the continuance of the amicable relations which existed between Russia and Great Britain. Thus Catherine, on her part, not only declined to renew the Anglo-Russian commercial treaty, but signed a commercial treaty with France in 1786 according her most-favoured-nation status, as a reward for France's abandoning her traditional friendship with the Turks.[18] On the other side, Pitt initiated an obstructive policy against Russia and in particular against French attempts to further their Black Sea commerce. It must also be pointed out that when war broke out between Russia and the Ottoman Empire in 1787, it was widely believed that Pitt and his Ambassador in Istanbul, Sir Robert Ainslie, were chiefly responsible.[19]

During the war the British trade, although still generally depressed began to develop in the newly-established settlement of Salonika in 1788. The trade flourished and became prosperous. Cloth, linen and muslins, tin, lead, raw and wrought iron and watches were sold there in exchange for cotton, tobacco and carpets.[20] Meanwhile, Russian and Austrian territorial expansion at the expense of the Ottoman Empire began, though slowly, to cause alarm in Britain. Towards the end of the war the Government began to see an interest in preserving the integrity of the Ottoman Empire.[21]

Towards the end of 1790, the British Government asked the Privy Council to submit a report on British trade in the Ottoman Empire. Having consulted the Levant merchants, the Privy Council submitted its long and interesting report to the Government.[22] It suggested that if British subjects were allowed to enter the Black Sea then it would be possible to develop a beneficial trade in the provinces bordering it, importing broadcloth, stuffs, muslins, calicos, all kinds of cotton goods, hardware, pottery, cotton hosiery, tin, lead, tin plates, coffee, sugar and copper in plates and exporting timber, hemp, hides, tallows and wax to Britain. It was thought that these articles, which were manufactured in Britain, would certainly be furnished at a much cheaper rate by British vessels if the latter were allowed to pass into the Black Sea. Furthermore, entrepôt trade might be carried out from the ports of Trabzon, Rize and Sinop to Iran, whereby British merchants might be able to buy fine Persian silk cheaper than it could be obtained through Izmir and Aleppo. It was also suggested that since the Ottoman vessels were not sufficiently advanced to cope with the rough Black Sea, then British subjects 'may instruct and improve the Ottomans in the arts of navigation'. The report went on to propose that the British be permitted to erect works, particularly saw-mills on the Black Sea or on rivers running into it. According to the Privy Council 'the state of Depression, to which this trade continues still to be subject, is to be imputed to improvident acts made by the Legislature to injudicious By Laws made by the Turkey Company, and to the delays occasioned by the present system of performing Quarantine'.[23]

However, the British Ambassador in Istanbul did not agree with this argument. In a despatch dated January 1791 he cited the expense involved in the navigation of British ships to the Black Sea, the restricted nature of the market which, in his view, English manufacturers would find there, and the inferior character of the raw materials that Britain could draw from the region. He argued that the British could import these raw materials from the Baltic much cheaper than from the Black Sea.[24]

In 1791, when discussing the integrity of the Ottoman Empire, a Member of Parliament declared that 'we may reasonably hope that soon the demand for our articles of exportation in Turkey will be very great, and we may count the Levant among the best markets our manufacturers have'.[25] Publishing a book at this time, David Sutherland also pointed out that:

> The Turks happily for us, are not a commercial people, notwithstanding their Empire has every advantage to induce them to become so. We cannot do without those valuable articles which their soil produces almost spontaneously, and the Turks, like the easy possessor of a very rich mine, allow us to enrich ourselves at our pleasure.[26]

An opponent of the Levant Company, F. Daniel, underlined this point in 1794:

> it is rather unfortunate for this country [i.e. Britain] that ancient factors were composed of a class of people so uninformed of the Products of Turkey, tho' the present Factors are not so ignorant, yet they are equally as unprofitable to this country, having established an indecent confidency to obstruct every New comer, thus a young man who has abilities and is ambitious to establish himself finds it impracticable, from a powerful combination and determined enmity, which he feels the severely, as he is ignorant of the cause.

He added that 'it is no wonder therefore that the Turkish Trade is so trifling', compared with 'the extent of the Ottoman dominions, the population, the various valuable productions which are equal if not superior to any European State'. Daniel concluded:

> At this period the Porte may be said to be in a situation, so as not to refuse anything and 'tho it may be ungenerous to take advantage of her, yet as she is totally ignorant of the nature of reciprocity and as it would be morally impossible to explain it to Her it can never be said an undue advantage was taken of her weakness, so unworthy the dignity of a Great Nation.[27]

However, the British trade continued to decline and once more the Levant Company had been compelled to apply to the Government for aid, which this was duly granted. The outbreak of war between France and Britain in 1793 produced a slump in the Company's trade. The worst period began in 1796 when Spain declared war on England; thus in 1797 no protection could be given to British merchants trading in the Mediterranean and this stagnant state of trade continued until Napoleon's invasion of Egypt in 1798.

A. C. Wood, the author of a book on the Levant Company, has remarked that several criticisms had been made of the Company's monopolistic nature. The critics of the Company always contended that the success of French competition and the diminution of British trade to the Levant were due to the errors of the Turkey Company and to its faulty organisation rather than to more general causes outside its control. It was believed that a handful of monopolists deliberately curbed all initiative, enterprise and expansion in pursuit of high profits on a limited business.[28]

Britain's trade had improved after Napoleon's Egyptian expedition in 1798, which led to the re-entry of the British fleet into the Mediterranean. Britain's naval victory made trade possible once more, while the struggle in Egypt increased the demand for British goods needed by the Ottomans to equip the armies they sent against the French invaders.[29] The unexpected attack on the Ottomans by France ended in a treaty between Britain and the Ottoman Empire in January 1799. By this treaty Britain obtained permission for her merchants to trade in the Black Sea region, but only after 1802. Corn, tallow and timber for naval purposes were the chief articles in which the British traded there when the old ban was lifted.[30]

After the invasion of Egypt by France, French trade in the Ottoman Empire was ruined. This was partly due to the decline in the quality of the cloth exported to the Empire by France as well as the increase in the export of shalloons, a closely woven woollen cloth chiefly used for linings, by the British. At the same time the dislocation of the trade routes in the Mediterranean due to the naval war with Britain seriously diminished the traffic between Marseilles and the Ottoman ports. The seizure of Egypt without any excuse or warning provoked the Porte into prohibiting all French trade in its ports. Thus, in the following years, the British had a unique opportunity to capture the Levant trade; so long as the war lasted the British possessed a virtual monopoly of Ottoman markets. British traders came to employ not only native ships and crews, but many which had once served in the merchant marines of Venice, Ragusa and Genoa.[31]

During the Anglo-French war of 1793 the Ottoman non-Muslim subjects, especially the Greeks, began to trade directly with the British, using their own ships. As this trade increased, the Levant Company's merchants considered that the Greeks would endanger their trade with the Ottoman Empire. According to the British merchants, if this practice were not stopped and serious measures taken by Britain, then the Ottoman subjects' trade would be detrimental to their own commerce and existence in the Levant. The British merchants in Izmir claimed that Ottoman subjects were allowed to trade directly with England only for a temporary period; although this period had expired, Greek merchants were still allowed to land their goods in Britain.[32] It was feared that, given the intriguing and deceitful character of the Greeks, they would soon not only establish commercial houses in London, as they did in Holland, but in time monopolise the trade to the utter exclusion of both British factories and merchants. For the Greek merchants were 'people so remarkably rash in commercial enterprise, so penurious in Domestic Life and so little scrupulous in means that no sober Merchant can possibly come in competition with them; and possessing so many advantages over us it would be utterly impossible to cope with them with any prospect of success'.[33] The British merchants in 1804 requested London completely 'to exclude Ottoman subjects of every description' and put the trade 'on the same footing as it existed upwards of a century ago'. They also explained to London that they had long stayed silent since their profit was very high and they could not be bothered to complain about the situation. Now, however, there was a risk that their advantage would pass to Ottoman subjects. The merchants claimed that they should naturally be allowed to reap the rewards of British industry.[34] When London reminded the merchants in Izmir to be very cautious, lest the Ottoman Government monopolise its foreign trade, they discounted the idea that the Porte would take such a step. Indeed, in 1802 the Ottoman Government took strong measures to protect its subjects trading abroad. The Porte established consulates in several cities in Europe in 1806 to protect its subjects' interests, but at the same time forbade non-Muslim subjects to trade under foreign protection.[35]

After the Industrial Revolution foreign goods poured into the Ottoman market. According to the capitulations, foreign merchants could only trade in the ports; internal markets were reserved for Ottoman subjects by the Ottoman Government. But foreign merchants found a way to penetrate the inland market without paying internal custom duties. Thus, the Ottoman treasury suffered. In 1802, the Ottoman Government sought to put an end to this practice. It asked British merchants to pay three per cent export and import duty plus the internal customs duties if they wanted to trade in internal markets. Acting jointly with his Russian colleague, the British Ambassador objected, claiming that British merchants were supposed to pay the internal custom duties, but only at a rate of three per cent. The conflict over this affair continued until 1806 when a new tariff was arranged.[36] Meanwhile a new Russo-Turkish war broke out in 1806; in 1807 Britain was dragged into it in support of Russia. The outbreak of war with the Ottomans hindered the expansion of British trade in the Ottoman Empire for a time. During the war, British merchants and their Consul-General moved to Malta, pending the restoration of peace. The favourable moment came for the British merchants when Napoleon was negotiating at Tilsit with the Russians for the partition of the Ottoman Empire. Knowing that Britain was not likely to share the Russian view, the Ottoman Government offered to negotiate peace terms with Britain in April 1808. The peace was signed at Çanakkale in January 1809.[37] By this treaty, Britain secured the restoration of the capitulations, while the Ottomans, in return, obtained the abolition of the old abuse of the ambassadors' *Berats*, or patents of protection. In addition British merchants anxious to trade into internal markets could do so on condition that they paid three per cent plus the internal custom duties.

The peace opened up a period of prosperity for British merchants. Indeed, during the Russo-Turkish war, British exports to the Ottoman Empire reached the highest figure recorded since the seventeenth century. Industrial products, particularly cotton goods, dominated the market. As Wood has emphasised, the new cotton goods, which were cheap, durable, bright in colour and light in weight, made an immediate appeal to the inhabitants of the country and swept aside the competition of similar textiles manufactured locally.[38]

In 1814 the Levant Company went so far as to say that:

> The desire for British manufactured goods which has been manifested by the subjects of the Porte of every description opens a door to an extension of our trade of the highest importance to this nation . . . and we have every reason to believe if those obstructions are removed, the demand will be prodigious.

At the same time, British colonial goods, such as sugar and coffee were pouring into the Ottoman Empire.[39]

It will be remembered that at the beginning of the nineteenth century new doctrines of economic liberalism were in the air. Industrial expansion created new conditions which threatened all economic monopolies. Accordingly, Britain's commercial interest in the Ottoman Empire could no longer be left to what Adam Smith described as 'a strict and oppressive monopoly'[40] of the Levant Company. In 1825 the Levant Company was dissolved and a new chapter started in the history of the Ottoman Empire.

In 1833, the then champion of Free Trade, Lord Palmerston, advised his Ambassador in Istanbul,[41] that in order to expand British interests both politically and economically, it would be necessary to end the Turkish monopolies, which in his view hindered British trade in the Ottoman Empire.[42] Finally, to his astonishment, in 1838 Lord Palmerston learned of the Porte's agreement to a treaty which enabled not only England but also the other European powers to enjoy free trade in the Ottoman Empire.

NOTES

1. A.C. Wood, *A History of the Levant Company*, (London, 1964) pp. 29, 41. cf., Mübahat S. Kütükoğlu, *Osmanlı-İngiliz İktisadi Münasebetleri I (1580–1838)*, (Ankara, 1974) p. 25.
2. Ibid., pp. 140–41. The average annual imports and exports for 1754–63 dropped to £130,028 and £71,327; in the following ten years they were £135,119 and £76,461, while between 1774 and 1783 they reached only £107,477 and £88,065.
3. Ibid., pp. 141, 161.
4. M.S. Anderson, 'Great Britain and the Russian Fleet, 1769–70', *Slavonic and Eastern European Review*, vol. 30 (1952) pp. 148–63; 'Great Britain and the Russo-Turkish War of 1768–1774', *English Historical Review*, vol. 69 (1954) pp. 38–58. See also Ali İhsan Bağış, 'The Embassy of Sir Robert Ainslie at Istanbul (1776–1794)' unpublished Ph.D. thesis, London Univ., 1974, pp. 17–18.
5. Wood, op. cit., p. 143.
6. P. Masson, *Histoire du commerce français dans le Levant au XVIII ième siècle* (Paris, 1911) pp. 412–16, 476–8.
7. Wood, op. cit., p. 161.
8. Bağış, op. cit., p. 147.

9. State Papers, 97/5, Ainslie to Weymouth, 3 February 1779. cf. Wood, op. cit., p. 147.
10. Ibid., pp. 158–59, 162.
11. M.S. Anderson, 'The Great Powers and the Annexation of the Crimea, 1783–84', *Slavonic and East European Review*, vol. 37 (1958–9) pp. 17–41; see also, Bağış, op. cit., pp. 30–45.
12. It was estimated that the Ottoman treasury annually lost £2000. Ainslie to Carmarthen, PRO, FO 78/10, 25 May 1784. cf. Başbakanlık Arşivi, İbn-ul Emin, Hariciye, no. 1571 and 1572.
13. The French merchants had enjoyed this privilege since 1740.
14. Ainslie to Carmarthen, PRO, FO 75/5, 10 November 1784.
15. See A.İ. Bağış, 'Rusların Karadeniz'de Yayılması Karşısında İngiltere'nin Ticari Endişeleri', in O. Okyar and H. İnalcık, eds., *Social and Economic History of Turkey (1071–1920)* (Ankara, 1980) pp. 211–12.
16. R. Willis, *A Short Account of the Crim-Tartary; and of the Imports and Exports*, (London, 1787).
17. H.J. Rose, *William Pitt and National Revival* (London, 1911); A.W. Ward and G.P. Gooch, *The Cambridge History of British Foreign Policy, 1783–1914*, vol. 1 (New York, 1922); J. Ehrman, *The Younger Pitt (The Years of Acclaim)* (London, 1969).
18. J. Ehrman, *The British Government and Commercial Negotiations with Europe, 1783–1793* (Cambridge, 1962).
19. For further details see, Bağış, 'The Embassy . . . '.
20. Wood, op. cit., p. 164.
21. A.İ. Bağış, 'The Advent of British Interests and the Integrity of the Ottoman empire', *Hacettepe University Bulletin of Social Sciences*, no. 1 (December 1978) pp. 102–18.
22. British Library, Add. MSS. 38394. See also Bağış, 'Rusların Karadeniz'de Yayılması Karşısında', p. 213.
23. Ibid.
24. Ainslie to Leeds, PRO, FO 78/12 A, 19 January 1791, cited in Bağış, 'The Advent of British Interests', p. 115.
25. Ibid., p. 111.
26. Captain David Sutherland, *A Tour up the Straits, from Gibraltar to Constantinople* (2nd ed., London, 1970) pp. 182–3.
27. British Library, Add. MSS. 38229, pp. 146–71.
28. Wood, op. cit., p. 150.
29. M.S. Anderson, *The Eastern Question, 1774–1923. A Study in International Relations* (London, 1966).
30. Wood, op. cit., pp. 180–1.
31. Ibid., p. 187.
32. A.I. Bağış, *III. Selim Devrinde Osmanlı İmperatorluğunda "Beratlı Avrupa Tüccarı" Meselesi*, unpublished *Doçent* thesis, Hacettepe University, March 1982.
33. Merchants to Levant Company. PRO SP 105/129, 13 July 1803, cited in Bağış, *III. Selim Devrinde, Beratlı Avrupa Tüccarı.*

34. Ibid., p. 74.
35. Ibid., p. 79 ff.
36. Ibid., pp. 81–93. See also Kütükoğlu, op. cit. pp. 64–5, 78–9.
37. Anderson, op. cit., pp. 38–45.
38. Wood, op. cit., p. 192.
39. Ibid., p. 193.
40. Adam Smith, *The Wealth of Nations*, ed. Edwin Cannan, vol. 2 (London, 1961) p. 258.
41. V.J. Puryear, *International Economics and Diplomacy in the Near East, 1834–1853* (California, 1969) p. 118.
42. Ibid.; F.E. Bailey, *British Policy in the Turkish Reform Movement, 1826–1853* (New York, 1970); Kütükoğlu, op. cit., pp. 86–125; see also, Charles Issawi, *The Economic History of Turkey, 1800–1914* (London, 1980).

V

THE OTTOMAN-BRITISH COMMERCIAL TREATY OF 1838

Mübahat Kütükoğlu

Relations between the Ottoman Empire and Britain began later than in the cases of some of the other European countries. Nevertheless, they developed speedily and continued in a friendly fashion for almost three and a half centuries up to the First World War. However, no matter how good the relations between any two states may be, it is a fact that both sides will safeguard their own interests. This can mean that decisions which may be harmful to the other side may be taken. The commercial treaty which was signed shortly before the beginning of the Tanzimat reforms on 16 August 1838 at Balta Limanı may serve as an example.

After the first privileges which were granted by Sultan Murat III to British merchants in 1580, which allowed them to trade in Ottoman territory, the treaty was renewed with each change of monarch up to 1675. Articles which improved and increased these privileges were added from time to time at the request of the British.[1] For example in 1601, less than twenty-five years after British merchants received the first contract, the customs duties they paid were lowered from five per cent to three per cent. The Austrians received the same right only in 1616, and the French in 1673.[2] Compared to the prosperity of the seventeenth century, British trade in the Levant seems to have slowed down somewhat in the eighteenth. It only began to revive towards the end of the century.[3] The contemporaneous Industrial Revolution increased the need for raw materials and new markets had to be developed for its products. The Ottoman Empire was regarded both as a supplier and as a market.

On the other hand the Empire also had a traditional commercial policy. Soon after the foundation of the Ottoman Empire the citizens of European countries were given trading privileges with a view to developing and encouraging commerce. But, in order to prevent the removal of food products and industrial raw materials from the country, restrictions were placed on exports: grains headed the list and were followed by cotton, cotton yarn, leather, morocco leather, wax, fine wool and mohair.[4] Although these goods could be exported with special permission in years when the crop was abundant or when its quality did not meet the requirements of domestic industry, the regulations which stated that foreign merchants could export every kind of goods they wanted provided that their export was not 'prohibited'[5] gave the Turkish Government the permanent right to place export bans on various items.

However, towards the end of the eighteenth century the attempts to reform the Ottoman Empire necessitated the development of new sources of government income. Among them was an increase in the customs rate which was described as 'the difference between the old and the new tariffs'.[6] In 1826, following the establishment of the new model army, and the abolition of the Janissary corps, the need for new sources of income to meet the expenses of this army arose. It was believed that if some of the crops were harvested directly by the Government and sold to foreign traders then the treasury would receive the difference between the purchase and selling prices. This system, which was referred to as *yed-i vahid*, or state monopoly, could provide substantial profits for the treasury if it were applied successfully.

As it was, these hopes were frustrated. The monopoly on silk and olive oil lasted only one or two years and the monopoly on grains for five to six years.[7] Although the government monopoly of the opium trade was the only one which was continued, the monopoly system displeased foreign merchants who preferred to buy products directly from the producer. This was especially true of the British, who needed to find new markets or improve the existing ones, due to the demands of the Industrial Revolution. Britain needed plentiful and cheap raw materials to maintain her production. Merchants of certain states, with whom special agreements had been signed, had the right to export unprohibited goods by paying customs duties of three per cent. To prevent them exporting goods without paying the domestic taxes, a *ferman* was issued to the effect that on such occasions foreign merchants would be subject to the same regulations as Ottoman citizens. At the beginning of the nineteenth century with the arrangement of the new customs duties with Britain, Russia and Austria on 21 October 1801 the problem of domestic trade was settled. The solution was laid down in Article 6 of the treaty of alliance of Kal'a-i Sultaniye of 1809 in the following terms: 'the British government accepts and undertakes the principles of the article on domestic trade'.[8]

To meet the expenses of the new army further measures were taken in 1826. The Octroi was readjusted, the range of cases in which it could be applied was increased, and extra items were included in the Izmir Octroi.[9] In addition to these impediments a special permit or *tezkire* was required for the transport of goods from one part of the country to another. Meanwhile Mehmet Ali Pasha, the Governor of Egypt, also enforced a system of state monopolies in Egypt, Syria and Crete. As a result, European merchants who had had high hopes for the future of their trade with the Ottoman Empire, were naturally displeased. Objections and complaints followed thick and fast.

Although the Ottoman Government tried to create new sources of income for its treasury, the rise in prices had the opposite effect. The customs rates were fixed for a long period of time – as long as fourteen years. For a short period before each readjustment, therefore, the real rate would drop to as low as 1–1.5 per cent, from the normal level of three per cent. The Ottoman Government thus sought to raise the tariffs as soon as they expired.[10] Such a situation arose in 1834 upon the expiry of the 1820 tariff. The British Foreign Office, however, regarded this proposal as an excellent opportunity to secure the abolition of those articles which irritated her merchants in the Ottoman Empire. In the course of his preliminary negotiations with the new Turkish Ambassador, Nuri Efendi, the British Foreign Secretary, Lord Palmerston, stated that 'since the British are a trading nation they would not accept any condition which may harm the trade'. During his later negotiations he stressed the 'mutual interests' of the two countries. In return for the readjustment of the customs duties, which had become due on 1 March 1834, the Ottoman Empire would abolish those regulations such as the *yed-i vahid*, the bans on exports, and the *tezkire* requirements which restricted the activities of British merchants.[11]

In requesting these adjustments the British were justified in terms of protecting their own interests. However, this request threatened the economic life of the Ottoman Empire, to whom Britain was now allied. In response to the insistence of the Ottoman Government, the British Foreign Office ordered the Ambassador, Lord Ponsonby, to start negotiations. The British had completed preparations for this during the previous two years, and the draft of the treaty, as prepared by Urquhart, was presented to Palmerston in the spring of 1836. According to Article 4 of this draft, all forms of monopoly and prohibition in the Ottoman Empire were to be removed and in return, 'taking into consideration the interests of the Turkish treasury', a customs tax of three per cent would be fixed.[12] Nevertheless, in the autumn of 1836, the Ottoman Government objected to many of the articles of this draft and informed the British that its only desire was the removal of the tariffs. The negotiations continued on and off during 1837 and 1838. However, every day which passed increased the customs debts due, which weakened the resistance of the Ottoman Government.

In time, the Sublime Porte was also persuaded that the system of state monopolies was not bringing in any great profits to the Government.[13] As it was, the system had not been applied in the way that had been planned. In 1837, during

Sultan Mahmud II's trip to Rumelia, the ban on the export of grains was removed and the *yed-i vahid* was now applied only in the case of the opium trade. The whole of the opium crop was not purchased by the state monopoly merchants because, in spite of the precautions which were taken, it was impossible to prevent smuggling. It was therefore assumed that if the system of state monopolies were to be abolished then the Government would not stand to lose too much. On the other hand, it might be harmful in the future if a specific article stating this abolition were included in treaties with foreign governments. Namık Pasha, who was sent to London as Ambassador Extraordinary, attached great importance to this point: in one of his articles he insisted that no such clause should be referred to in any treaty.[14]

During 1830, the Ottoman Government also had to deal with their rebellious Governor, Mehmet Ali Pasha. To halt his armies it needed the political support of the European powers. The need for this political support also played an important role in the acceptance by the Ottoman Government of the conditions of the Treaty of Balta Limanı. The British Foreign Office made full use of this opportunity and persuaded the Sublime Porte that if the *yed-i vahid* were abolished throughout the Empire, then Mehmet Ali Pasha would be seriously weakened since he met most of the expenses of his army and navy by means of the state monopolies which were applied in Egypt and Syria.[15] As a result, under Article 2 of the commercial treaty signed on 16 August 1838 all the bans on exports were removed except for the *yed-i vahid* as it applied to agricultural products and certain other goods. In addition, the *tezkire* system was totally abandoned. Under Article 3, British merchants were given the same rights as Ottoman citizens. The basic principles of the customs tariff were laid out in Article 4. According to this regime, the customs duties on exports and imports remained at three per cent and the Ottoman Government undertook to abolish all domestic taxes on exported goods. In return it would receive a tax of nine per cent referred to as the *amediyye*. This tax would be paid by either domestic or foreign merchants, depending on who transported the goods from the region where they were produced to the export port.

Article 5 concerned permission for ships passing through the Straits, while Article 6 confirmed that the treaty was to cover all the Ottoman dominions including Egypt. The customs tariffs were referred to in Article 7 and included the principle that they would remain valid for seven years.

The second section of the treaty contained three Articles including regulations affecting the taxes paid on imported goods and on goods in transit. It made it clear that British merchants could trade in goods imported by other merchants provided they paid a three per cent customs duty and two per cent in other taxes. They were then entitled to buy and sell these goods without further taxation.[16]

As will have become clear, the treaty of 1838 provided great opportunities and freedom to British merchants trading in the Ottoman Empire but deprived the Ottoman treasury of a substantial source of income. It was decided that the treaty was to become valid as from 1 March 1839: in the event however it only entered into force the following July due to delay in adjustment of the customs tariffs.[17] After its entry into force points which had escaped the attention of the Ottoman delegation raised more serious problems than those which had been referred to openly in the treaty. From the very beginning, the British Foreign Office had requested that British merchants should have the right to conduct not only wholesale but also retail trade in the Empire.[18] However the British believed that it would be unwise to provoke anxieties on the part of the Ottoman delegation by stating this desire at the outset, since there were a large number of other unsolved problems. This point was therefore worked into the treaty between Article 3 of the main text and Article 2 of the Appendix. Sir Henry Bulwer, who had put in a great deal of effort during the preparation of the treaty, explained the gains which he looked for in a letter which he sent to Ambassador Ponsonby. He stated that besides Article 2, which referred to the right to trade in goods produced in Turkey, there was also an opportunity for merchants to enter the retail trade. His explanation of Article 2 of the Appendix, with reference to Article 3, pointed out that it might be possible to engage in the retail sale of both imported and home produced goods which were consumed in the Ottoman Empire.[19]

Not long after the treaty entered into force, the Sublime Porte had to face the bitter truth. The Ottoman Government tried to explain in vain that the right to commercial transactions referred only to wholesale trade and that the retail market was reserved for Ottoman subjects.[20] Although the Ottoman Government, which had gained some useful experience from its treaty with the British, succeeded in softening to some extent the conditions of the commercial treaty signed with the Russians in 1846, the British did not accept any changes in their treaty. The new commercial treaty signed in 1861 brought nothing new either as regards the monopolies or retail trade. In fact, the Ottoman Government, in signing these treaties, was even obliged to alter some of the regulations affecting its own citizens.

The adjustment of the customs tariff, which the Ottoman Government had been trying to renew since 1834 was only completed some time after the conclusion of the treaty. The reason for this delay was the desire of the British to establish the prices of goods produced in the Ottoman Empire in order to fix the export tariffs correctly. Hence, the taxes on imported goods were established first. There was also some debate about which regions should be used as the basis for the establishment of domestic prices and hence of the customs duties. The British had pressed for a reduction of the currently quoted prices: as a result, customs duties were established on the basis of the average prices for the previous five years. This disagreement between the delegates resulted in a delay to the implementation of the new tariffs, until the following July.

Following the Treaty of Balta Limanı[21] the Ottoman Government was unable to secure the changes which it wanted in the treaty. When the 1839 tariff came up for renewal in 1850, the Ottoman Government accepted a reduction of twenty per cent in the tariff on imports and sixteen per cent in that on exports.[22] Under the tariff of 1862 this ratio was reduced to ten per cent in both cases.[23] The commercial treaty of 1861, which established the tariff charged as from 1862, changed the customs policy completely. While import duties were raised to some extent, export duties were reduced by one per cent every year until they reached a low point of one per cent.

Although the Treaty of Balta Limanı limited the Sublime Porte's right to regulate her citizens and her ability to raise new revenue, it was not responsible for the downfall of the Ottoman Empire, as some historians have tried to prove. However, it is true that the treaty speeded up the process of decline. The corruption of the Empire had begun during the eighteenth century and increased after 1838. Had the suggestions of such advisers as the Customs Counsellor Tahir Bey or Namık Pasha been heeded then it might have been possible to prepare a treaty on more favourable terms and to slow down the economic decline, if not actually halt it.

NOTES

1. The treaties signed by the Ottomans from 1580 onwards can be found in *Mecmua-ı Muâhedat*, I (Istanbul 1294).
2. Halil İnalcık, 'İmtiyazat', *Encyclopedia of Islam*, new edition, III (Leiden, 1972) pp. 1185–6.
3. Britain became the chief rival of France after she received capitulations from the Ottoman Government in 1580. For details see, M.S. Kütükoğlu, *Osmanlı – İngiliz İktisadi Münasebetleri*, I. (Ankara, 1974) p. 38 ff.
4. Cereal grains were for public consumption and the others were for industrial use. These were only to be exported by special permission of the Government; there are many government prohibitions in the *Divan-ı Hümâyûn Defters*. Some of these documents are published in A. Rafik, *On Altıncı Asırda İstanbul Hayatı, 1583–1591*, (Istanbul 1935) pp. 120, 129, 131; Lütfi Güger, 'XVI. yüzyıl sonlarında Osmanlı İmperatorluğu dahilinde hububat ticaretinin tâbi olduğu kayıtlar' *İktisat Fakültesi Mecuması*, XIII/I-4 (Istanbul, 1953) p. 79 ff.
5. Kütükoğlu, op. cit., p. 23.
6. Başbakanlık Arşivi (hereafter cited as Bşb. Ar.), Cevdet tasnifi – Maliye nr. 28843.
7. Kütükoğlu, op. cit., p. 68.
8. *Mecmua-ı Muâhedat*, I. 268.
9. Kütükoğlu, op. cit., p. 81.
10. V.J. Puryear, *International Economics and Diplomacy in the Near East* (U.S.A. n.p. 1969) p. 119.

11. Palmerston to Nuri Efendi: *Bşb. Ar., Hatt-ı Hümâyûn*, nr 33015 - 1; see also Public Record Office (hereafter, FO), 78/268, pp. 81–3.
12. FO 78/2298, 18 May 1836. See also, Kütükoğlu, op. cit., pp. 92–4.
13. Hatt-ı Humâyûn, nr. 46365.
14. Report by Namık Paşa dated 5 Müharram 1251 (3 May 1835): *Hatt-ı Humâyûn*, nr. 61905-C.
15. Kütükoğlu, op. cit., I, pp. 101–2.
16. The treaty signed by Queen Victoria can be found in Bşb. Ar., Yabancı Devletlerle Yapılmış Muahede Orijinalleri, nr. 199 and 200; J.C. Hurewitz, *Diplomacy in the Near and Middle East: Documentary Record 1535–1914*, I (London, 1958) pp. 110–11; *Mecmua-ı Muâhedat*, 1, pp. 272–7.
17. Kütükoğlu, op. cit., II, (Istanbul, 1974).
18. Palmerston to Ponsonby 27 June 1837 FO 78/350; Denis de Marchant to Backhouse, 13 June 1837, FO 78/326.
19. FO 78/332, p. 153; see also Kütükoğlu, op. cit., I, pp. 110–13.
20. For further details see Kütükoğlu, op. cit., II, 83.
21. Ibid., p. 96.
22. M.S. Kütükoğlu, 'Tanzimat Devri Osmanlı-İngiliz Gümrük Tarifeleri', *Tarih Enstitüsü Dergisi*, no. 4–5 (Istanbul, 1974) pp. 340–3.
23. Ibid., pp. 344–8.

VI

TURCO-BRITISH RELATIONS IN THE INTER-WAR PERIOD: FETHI OKYAR'S MISSIONS TO LONDON

Osman Okyar

The purpose of this paper is to illustrate the dramatic reversal in the relations between Great Britain and Turkey during the period between the end of the First World War and the period prior to the Second World War by describing two diplomatic missions undertaken in the name of the Ankara National Government, by Fethi Okyar, first as Minister of the Interior of the Ankara Government in August 1922, and subsequently as Ambassador of the Turkish Republic between 1934 and 1938.

As an historical background to the events during the inter-war period, I survey very broadly in the first section of the paper the course of relations between the Ottoman and the British Empires during the nineteenth century, until 1914, when they found themselves fighting each other, Britain on the side of the Allies, while the Ottoman Empire had joined the ranks of the Entente powers. Open enmity thus broke a long period of peace and good relations. Subsequently British designs over the succession to the Ottoman Empire in the Middle East and in South-East Europe provided the motivations behind its attitude towards the national movement established by Atatürk, in Ankara, in April 1920.

A year after the Turkish forces under Atatürk had stopped the advance of the Greek army into Anatolia on the Sakarya, Atatürk sent Fethi Okyar, on a mission to London in August 1922, to find out whether the British Government was willing to consider favourably peace terms which would lead to Turkish independence and to the withdrawal of the Greek army, without further warfare between Greeks and Turks. Although the mission failed in its declared aim, Fethi Okyar was successful in putting Turkey's case to British and western public opinion and in winning understanding for Turkey. The failure of Fethi Okyar's mission, which is described in the second section of the paper, was followed by the Turkish counter-offensive of August 1922 which led to the expulsion of the Greek army from Anatolia and to the Lausanne Peace Treaty in 1923. The third section of the paper takes up relations in the inter-war period which remained cool until the early years of the 1930s.

However, Turkey's admission into the League of Nations in 1932 marked, in a sense, the end of her isolation from the international community and the beginning of new initiatives in foreign affairs. In the thirties, the decisive events which influenced the Turkish Government on one side and the Western powers, Great Britain and France, on the other, to come closer together, was the growing menace of German expansionism, accompanied by the Italian moves towards annexing Ethiopia.

The relations which developed between Turkey and the Western powers during the second half of the thirties were to culminate in the Treaty of Alliance signed in Ankara in 1939, between Turkey, Great Britain and France. This move, which signalled a return to the friendship of the nineteenth century and also involved the cooling of the previous close relations between the Soviet Union and Turkey, was mainly dictated by strategic and geo-political considerations. However, the role of diplomats also played a part in this process. I have in mind friendly contacts established in Britain by Fethi Okyar, Turkish Ambassador in London between 1933 and 1939, on the one side and in Turkey by Sir Percy Loraine, the British Ambassador in Ankara between 1934 and 1939 on the other. The third and final section of the paper deals with developments in Turkish foreign policy during the time of Fethi Okyar's ambassadorship in London between 1934 and 1939.

The nineteenth century opened with a long period (1830–1880) during which relations between the British Empire and the Ottoman Empire were very close. However, relations cooled somewhat towards the end of the century. In 1914, the two powers found themselves fighting on opposite sides during the First World War. The main motive behind the growing friendship between Britain and the Ottoman Empire during the nineteenth century was political, namely to prevent a Russian southward advance. The desire to maintain the territorial integrity of the Empire against the Russian threat led the Ottoman statesmen of the *Tanzimat* to look to Britain, as the leader of the West and the foremost naval world power. On the other hand, the British Empire was vitally interested in keeping intact its links with India and the Far East. Russia was the main power threatening to cut the link in the middle.

The nineteenth century movement of reform and modernisation within the Ottoman Empire, known as the *Tanzimat*, had the active backing and support of the West, led by Great Britain, because the liberal West thought that modernisation in a European direction would strengthen the Empire, politically, economically and militarily. In addition to the intrinsic worth of the reform, representing a move from a non-western state and society towards the higher valued system of the West and its rational world outlook, the West hoped that reform would strengthen the Empire so as to enable it to act as a counterweight to Russia. On the other hand, the amorphous Russian Empire was more ambivalent, even sometimes hostile to the Ottoman reform movement, which was considered to be a process which might eventually strengthen a state and society which the Russians really wanted to dismember.

An early instrument used by the Russians in order to penetrate into the Empire and influence its policies was religion. Russia offered protection and inspiration to Ottoman subjects of the Orthodox faith (around twelve million), on the pretence that they were maltreated and persecuted by the Ottomans. The excuse of religious persecution was the pretext behind the Russian army's advance into Ottoman territory in 1853, after the Ottomans rejected the Russian ultimatum demanding to be given officially the title of Protector of the Orthodox Faith and the conclusion of a treaty of alliance between Russia and Turkey. This Russian aggression led to Britain and France coming to the help of the Ottomans in the Crimean War, which ended in Russian defeat and in the Treaty of Paris of 1856, when all the European Powers guaranteed Ottoman territorial integrity.

After failing to use religion as a successful instrument of division, the Russians turned towards racism and nationalism, as more powerful instruments to break up the Ottoman domination in southern Europe. The dream of uniting all the Slavs living in the Balkans and in Eastern Europe, in a federation to be led by Russia, was encouraged by the pan-Slav movement based in Moscow. Panslavism was accompanied by the encouragement of nationalist tendencies. Propaganda and agitation brought about a period of troubles in the Balkans, between 1870 and 1875. Around the same time, the emerging movement of the Young Ottomans who grew impatient with the time-consuming *Tanzimat* evolution, started pressing for political reform within the Ottoman Empire, designed to bring about a parliamentary monarchy along constitutional lines. One of the purposes of the Young Ottomans was to bolster the new identity of Ottomanism throughout the Empire. The allegiance to Ottomanism would, it was hoped, embrace equally all Ottoman subjects, irrespective of nationality, race and religion. Equal representation in parliament was seen as the solution for many conflicts within the multi-racial state, with the objective of making unnecessary the demands for independence or autonomy coming from within the Empire.

However, troubles and conflicts in the Balkans, which Russia encouraged, particularly in Serbia, Herzegovina and Bulgaria, came to a head around 1876. The Russians had convinced all major European continental powers, with the exception of Great Britain, to present to the Empire the so-called Berlin Memorandum, demanding foreign diplomatic supervision over the reform measures and the granting of an amnesty to Serbs and Bulgars, who had revolted and made war against the Ottoman state. With the Berlin Memorandum still unanswered, the British proposed an international conference to meet in Istanbul, to review the Balkan crisis. The timing of the conference coincided with the proclamation by Sultan Abdülhamid II of the constitution prepared by the Grand-Vizier Midhat Paşa and his followers. The euphoric feelings created by the constitution played a part in the decision of the Ottoman Government to reject the resolution of the Istanbul international conference, asking the Ottomans to enlarge somewhat the frontiers of the independent states of Serbia and Montenegro and to grant autonomy to Bosnia, Herzegovina and Bulgaria. The British advice to accept these recommendations was ignored by the Ottomans.

The Russians quickly used the Ottoman rejection to cross over into Turkish territory, in April 1877. The British did not take part in the Russian-Turkish war on the Ottoman side, as the Ottoman Government seemed to have hoped. They contented themselves with sending a fleet to the waters near the straits, to prevent a Russian occupation of Istanbul. After their disastrous defeat at the hands of the Russians in the 1877–1878 war, the Ottomans gave up very large areas of territory in Europe to the independent states of Montenegro, Serbia, and Romania. They also granted autonomy to Bulgaria, through the Treaty of Berlin in July 1878.

Relations between Britain and Turkey in the latter part of the nineteenth century, between 1880 up to the open enmity in 1914, were on the surface friendly, but never as close as they had been between 1830 and 1880. The main factor which brought about changes in the substance and in the tone of these relations was that, on the Turkish side, the attitude towards Britain of Sultan Abdülhamid II, who held final responsibility for decision making, seemed to have cooled considerably relatively to the past, for a number of reasons.

The annexation of Cyprus by Britain following the Berlin Treaty and the British occupation of the nominally Ottoman province of Egypt in 1882, shook the confidence of Abdülhamid in Britain as the principal power capable of ensuring the territorial integrity of the Ottoman Empire. He turned to other policies and options to buttress the Empire. Two shifts were in particular noticeable:

1. Efforts to win over the friendship and allegiance of Arabs and Indians belonging to the Islamic faith. The aim was to work towards a pan-Islamic federation which would bring together all Muslims throughout the world. The special care given to the Holy Places in Palestine and Arabia, the construction of the Damascus to Mecca pilgrimage railway were symbolic actions in this respect. Abdülhamid's policy of pan-Islamism was bound to attract the suspicion of the British Empire, which had millions of Muslim subjects in India, Egypt and the Arab world.

2. The shift in Ottoman foreign and economic policies towards Germany, which was becoming the leading military and economic power on the continent. The growing German power was increasingly looked upon to replace Britain as the major power capable of guaranteeing the territorial integrity of the Ottoman state against Russian expansion.

On the other hand, in the late nineteenth century, certain shifts in the British attitude towards Turkey were also to be noted. First there was a growing body of opinion in England, especially within the Liberal Party, which had turned strongly anti-Turkish on allegedly moral grounds. Puritanism and humanitarian feelings, whipped up by one-sided press reports of so-called Turkish atrocities perpetrated against the Christian peoples in the Balkans and against the Armenians, were the main fuel behind this rise of anti-Turkish feelings. Gladstone, the head of the Liberal Party which came to power in England in 1880, referred to the 'terrible Turks who ought to be forever expelled from Europe'.

Changes in the balance of power in Europe also tended to put into the background one of the main objectives of British policy in the nineteenth century, which had been to support the Ottoman state as a bulwark against Russian penetration into the Middle East and the Mediterranean. In British eyes, the fear of imperial Germany's domination over Europe had, by the early twentieth century, tended to replace the fear of Russian expansionism. This led to a *rapprochement* between

Britain and Russia. Moreover, the newly acquired British territories in Egypt and Cyprus led some British statesmen to consider the Ottoman state as expendable and to turn to the alternative solution of dividing up the moribund Ottoman Empire between the Great Powers.

When the Young Turk revolution swept Abdülhamid from power and restored the Constitution in 1908, there was a resurgence of interest in Western Europe among the pro-Western young Turks. Hopes increased that Britain and France would be more sympathetic towards an Islamic Empire, struggling to establish constitutional democracy. However, these rather naïve ideas were soon to be undermined by geo-political factors, which dictated a *rapprochement* between the Western powers and Russia, against the threat of German domination over Europe.

Could the Ottoman Empire have remained neutral in the looming conflict between the two European blocks? Within the leaders of the Union and Progress Party, there were some, such as Mustafa Kemal and Fethi Okyar, who were against the Ottoman Empire taking sides between the polarising forces in Europe. But they were not in positions of power, while Enver Pasha, the leader of the triumvirate ruling Turkey, was leaning towards the Germans, partly under the influence of Panturanian ideas which looked towards an eventual union of Turks and Turkic peoples, after the hoped for break-up of the Russian Empire.

Turkey's destiny was no longer completely in her own hands, however, since the Turkish armed forces had to rely on foreign support for modernisation and for weapons. In 1913, the German Ambassador in Istanbul, Mangenheim, wrote to his Government the following words: 'The power which controls the army in Turkey will be supreme. As long as we control the Army, no anti-German government can long remain in power.' Thus, the Ottoman Government could remain neutral for only three months after the outbreak of hostilities in the First World War. As a consequence of what is considered a *fait accompli*, engineered by Germany, the Ottoman Empire found itself fighting Russia on one front and the British Empire on another, in October 1914.

With the above developments in mind, it is possible to agree only partly with the commonly-accepted view that during the nineteenth century foreign help was sought only for particular purposes and was not regarded as a permanent factor in the making of Ottoman foreign policy. In this regard the Empire's participation in a military alliance with the Central Powers in 1914 was, it is true, an *ad hoc* decision, but its outcome discouraged further improvisations of this sort.

We turn now to the state of Turco-British relations at the end of the First World War, when the victorious European Allies, with Britain at their head, were sharing out the spoils of the Ottoman defeat. Allied armies were busy occupying various parts of Turkish territory, but the gravest threat to the survival of the Turkish nation came when the Greek army landed in Izmir, in May 1919, in a move which had been sanctioned by the Allied Supreme Council in Paris, but, had been in reality prepared between Lloyd George and Venizelos, the British and Greek Prime Ministers. This British move indicated a complete reversal of the traditional British policy of the nineteenth century, which had been to support the existence and integrity of the Ottoman state, as a barrier against the southward expansion of the Russian Empire. Now, after its victory in the war and the collapse of the old Russian Empire, followed by the establishment of what appeared then a weak Bolshevik state in Russia, Britain seemed to be thinking that in the future western security in the Middle East and the Mediterranean could be maintained without an essential Turkish contribution. In this new line of thinking, the security formerly provided by Turkey would be partly supplied by an extended Greek state, owning a large slice of Western Anatolia, on one side, and partly by the British and French presence and domination in the former territories of the Ottoman Empire in the Middle East, on the other.

The Greek landings in Izmir and the Allied dismissal of the Turkish Parliament which met in Istanbul in 1919, were key moves which reinforced tremendously the new national movement established in Ankara by Mustafa Kemal. The new Turkish Government proved strong enough to throw back the onslaught of the Greek army on the Sakarya River near Ankara in August 1921. Preparations began afterwards for a Turkish counter-offensive, which would finally break the back of the Greek army and throw the Greeks out of Anatolia. During the long lull which set in in the fighting between the Greeks and Turks after September 1921, the Turkish Government reached separate agreements with Britain's allies, France and Italy over their recognition of Turkish sovereignty over disputed areas in Anatolia, which the Turks said came within the boundaries set by the National Pact in 1919. However, Great Britain continued to back the Greek move into Anatolia and appeared opposed to any discussion of peace terms with the Turkish nationalist government, on the basis of Turkish sovereignty, within the boundaries of the National Pact.

What were, at that time, the precise outlines of British thinking as regards future arrangements in Asia Minor? Was Britain at all ready to recognise, without further fighting, the boundaries set down in the National Pact and to use its influence over the Greeks to get them to withdraw from Anatolia? What were the lines of British thinking over other points of the future peace treaty with Turkey? These were the key things Atatürk wanted to know before deciding to launch a final counter-offensive against the Greeks. In case of an expected negative response from Britain, he also wanted to show to world opinion that the onus of responsibility for continued warfare in Asia Minor lay with Great Britain and Greece, and not with the Turks.

The mission in the Allied capitals of Paris and London of Yusuf Kemal Tengirşenk, the Foreign Minister of the Ankara Government, undertaken in March 1922, aimed at discovering and probing Allied and British intentions. The subsequent mission of Fethi Okyar to London in August 1922 had the objective of pinning down responsibility for the war on the British Government and winning over world opinion to Turkey's side. The negative result of Tengirşenk's mission is described in his memoirs published in 1967.[1] Thus, on 21 March, he was received by the British Foreign Secretary, Lord Curzon, to whom he explained the point of view of the Turkish Government when asking for the recognition of the frontiers laid down in the National Pact of 1919. Tengirşenk further explained that such a recognition was not, in any way, counter to British interest in the region. Curzon replied that Britain was willing to alter some of the provisions of the Sèvres Treaty, in the following ways:

1. Guarantees for protecting the rights of minorities in Turkey would be demanded.

2. A regime of neutrality would be imposed upon the Straits, over which full sovereignty would not be given back to Turkey.

3. A special regime, around the Izmir area, taking account of the Greek presence in Western Anatolia, was foreseen.

Although departing from the extremes of the Sèvres Treaty, the points made by Curzon indicated extensive restrictions on Turkish sovereignty, as foreseen in the National Pact. Neither such demands, nor the ceasefire offer of the Western allies to Turkey and Greece, made on 22 March 1922, proposing the creation of arbitrating allied military commissions with the Turkish and Greek armies in the field, could be accepted.

The outcome of the Tengirşenk mission had been to convince Atatürk that hopes of a peaceful solution with Britain and Greece were non-existent. However, before ordering the final counter-offensive, he decided on sending yet another mission to London, this time to be headed by his trusted friend Fethi Okyar, with quite different objectives. The words in which Fethi Okyar described Atatürk's approach towards this last mission are as follows:

> I have decided to launch soon the counter-offensive. But my purpose is to prove to my own country and to the world that we still want peace, if it can be obtained on the terms of the National Pact. We know that the British will refuse such terms, but world opinion must be openly informed about our case. This is the sense of your London mission. Another objective is to gain time and

> deceive the English and the Greeks into thinking that we are still trying to reach agreement with them.[2]

In London, Fethi Okyar stayed at the Savoy Hotel and after arrival, went to the Foreign Office to present his credentials. He asked for an interview with Lord Curzon. He was told that his request would be transmitted to the Foreign Secretary and the reply delivered to the hotel. On the third day of his stay in London, came a message from Mustafa Kemal, asking him to continue with his work, which was to be interpreted as to continue to gain time. He then decided to call a press conference at the hotel, on the subject of Turkish rights in the context of the forthcoming peace in the Middle East. In this well-attended press conference, Fethi Okyar began by saying that he had returned to Turkey a short time ago from Malta, where he had been held for two years as a British prisoner. He explained that no serious divergence of interests existed between Britain and Turkey, either on historical or on geopolitical grounds. He added that the present British Government seemed motivated by the desire to punish the Turkish nation. This first press conference found a wide echo within the British press.

Meanwhile, the Foreign Secretary instructed his Permanent Under-Secretary to receive Atatürk's representative on 14 August 1922. Fethi Okyar again presented Turkey's case to the Under-Secretary, who said he would transmit it to Lord Curzon. Fethi Okyar also asked whether it was useful for him to remain much longer in London, since his mission involved establishing contacts with the British Government. Mustafa Kemal was immediately informed of the developments and his answer arrived on 16 August: 'Continue to gain time. Repeat everywhere that we are ready to sit down at the peace table, together with the British. Take special care of the media. The date which you know about has not been changed'.

Fethi Okyar then proceeded to organise a second press conference at the Savoy Hotel; he invited not only the representatives of British papers, but also correspondents of the foreign press in London, the press attachés of foreign embassies and a representative of Indian Muslims. In his statement, he again stressed that Turkey's objectives went no further than asking for honourable and equitable terms for self-determination. He vigorously attacked the British Government in the following terms: 'Please question me about Turkish objectives. On the basis of my answers, enquire from responsible British statesmen, their views on the matter, so as to inform world opinion about the truth.'

Fethi Okyar's plan succeeded. The next day, not only the British papers, but foreign news media also, carried reports of the Turkish call to peace. The Opposition in the House of Commons asked Lord Curzon about his views on the statement of the Turkish representative. An Opposition MP in the House of Commons asked the Government why Lord Curzon had kept him waiting for fourteen days granted that he was a Minister of the Ankara Government, who was also a well-known Turkish statesman. The next day, on 25 August 1922, Fethi Okyar was again received by the Permanent Under-Secretary at the Foreign Office who gave him the following message from Lord Curzon: 'The Foreign Secretary is working on the problems outstanding between the two countries and he will receive you in the first week of September, when he will have completed his preparations.'

The Turkish counter-offensive began on the morning of 26 August, and on 28 August the French news agency Havas carried a report that Afyon had been retaken by the Turks and that the Turkish army was advancing westwards. On 30 August, Curzon's personal secretary telephoned the Savoy Hotel to tell Fethi Okyar that the Foreign Secretary wanted to see him immediately. It was only from this hurried meeting that Fethi Okyar learnt about the total Greek defeat and the capture of the Greek Commander-in-Chief. Curzon then asked Fethi Okyar to enquire whether Ankara was ready for a cease-fire to stop further bloodshed and prevent more destruction in Western Anatolia. He also asked him to inform him about the reply, irrespective of the time. Fethi Okyar sent a cipher message to Atatürk, informing him of the British request. He suggested that France and Italy would not move to help the Greek army. He proposed that in her reply to the British, Turkey should demand the return of Thrace, the exchange of minorities between Greece and Turkey, and a war indemnity. He also suggested that she should fully inform European public opinion about recent Greek atrocities and destructions in Anatolia.

Sensing that the Turkish reply to the British demand for a ceasefire would be late in coming, Fethi Okyar decided to leave London and return home via Paris and Rome, 6 September 1922. But before he left, he attended the House of Commons debate on foreign policy, in the course of which it had been announced that Prime Minister Lloyd George would make a statement; Ramsay MacDonald, speaking for the Labour Opposition, asked whether the Prime Minister was still intent on following a policy, the consequences of which he had been warned about many times. Lloyd George replied evasively, stressing that Britain had always remained loyal to her word, whatever the consequences. He added that he had asked Turkey to refrain from carrying military operations into the region around the Straits. Upon being asked by an Opposition MP what he would do if the Turks entered the Straits region in defiance of the British request, Lloyd George replied, half evasively, half menacingly, that he did not think Ankara would act in this fashion.

So, the first mission undertaken by Fethi Okyar to reopen British-Turkish relations, just before the end of the Turkish war of Independence, was not immediately successful in bringing the British and the Turks around to the discussion table. However, the mission achieved the important objectives of informing world opinion about Turkish peace terms, of gaining time for Ankara and of deceiving the enemy about the impending Turkish counter-offensive.

The point from which relations between Turkey and Great Britain began to develop in the inter-war period was the long period of open and concealed warfare between 1914 and 1923. It is not surprising that the early phase in these relations, up to the early thirties, was marked by a certain coolness and by lingering hesitations on both sides.

Long before Turkey was precipitated into the First World War on the German side, Atatürk had nurtured the ambition of rising to a position of power in Turkey, from which he would propel his country radically in a European direction. Even when fighting against the Greeks and against Western plans to divide Turkey, Atatürk did not give up his basic hopes and his conceptions of westernisation, during the war of Independence. Memories of the fighting and signs of resentment towards the West faded rapidly in Atatürk's mind after Lausanne. For a time, his main concern was to establish equality of status and of legal rights as between the new Turkish Republic and European states.

Following the Lausanne Treaty, relations between Great Britain and Turkey were clouded for a number of years by the conflict over Mosul. This was to be settled in 1926 by a League of Nations arbitration judgment in favour of Britain. The admission of Turkey into the League of Nations in 1931, the improvement in Turkey's relations with her Balkan neighbours (above all with Greece) and the revision of the regime of the Straits in Turkey's favour through the Montreux Convention of 1936 were indications of the growth of a climate of confidence between Turkey and the Western European powers.[3] However, the main factors which brought about much closer relations between Britain and Turkey, culminating in the credit arrangements signed in London in 1938 and in the Treaty of Alliance signed in Ankara in 1939, were the increasing dangers of European security posed by Italian and German expansionism.

It appears that Atatürk's desire to strengthen Turkey's ties with Britain began in the early thirties. The story is related by Sir Percy Loraine, the British Ambassador in Ankara between 1934 and 1939. At the end of the long game of poker played after a banquet given in June 1934, in Ankara, in honour of the Shah of Iran, Atatürk took the Ambassador aside and expressed to him his wish for friendship with England. He proposed to wipe out all the bitter memories since 1914 and start again as good and trusted friends. The Ambassador replied that there was no reason why relations should not become better and speaking of Turkey's alliance with Russia, assured the President that this would be no barrier to a parallel friendship with Britain.[4]

Another sign of Atatürk's early interest in developing better relations with Britain was the appointment of his friend Fethi Okyar as Ambassador in London in 1934. Fethi Okyar had been brought back by Atatürk from his post of Ambassador in Paris in July 1930, in order to form an opposition party to succeed what had been a *de facto* single party rule by the People's Republican Party in Turkey, between 1925 and 1930. Atatürk had always wanted to establish in Turkey a multi-party framework, within which the Government and the opposition parties, although agreeing on the main principles of the Republican regime and of the Constitution of 1924, would nevertheless differ on political and economic questions. So Fethi Okyar accepted the job of forming a new opposition party in July 1930 to be named the Liberal Party. But it turned out soon that the prevailing political, social and psychological conditions in Turkey were not yet ripe enough to make the experiment of multi-party democracy possible. So the experiment in multi-party democracy was terminated in November 1930.

Fethi Okyar was highly disillusioned by this outcome but his friendship with Atatürk did not suffer from the experiment. He did not stand for re-election in the parliamentary election of 1931 and went to Istanbul to lead a life of retirement, devoted to reading and writing. His appointment early in 1934 as Ambassador in London, was another sign of the growing importance of Turkish-British ties in the eyes of Atatürk.

Fethi Okyar had begun to study English as a prisoner of war in Malta during the years 1919 to 1921. His understanding of the language had then developed enough to enable him to translate into Turkish the book by Maynard Keynes, *The Economic Consequences of the Peace*. This translation was subsequently published in Turkey. However, his vocabulary and speaking practice had remained somewhat deficient. One of his first moves in London was to buy a set of English linguaphone records to which he regularly listened, until he was able to speak the language quite easily. He and his wife soon entered London society where they became very popular. Fethi Okyar liked to listen to the House of Common debates, since he had always been a believer in political democracy. He got acquainted with a number of British politicians. Thus, the old Prime Minister and former foe of Turkey, Lloyd George once received him in his home. He also met Winston Churchill, whom he greatly admired and who was then a lonely opponent of the ruling Conservative Party wing, under Baldwin.

The social side of Fethi Okyar's mission to London was complemented by political and diplomatic activity designed to develop the relationship between Britain and Turkey. The Turkish Ambassador had always essentially been a believer in western pluralism and in multi-party democracy. He detested all forms of totalitarianism, whether of the National Socialist or of the Communist variety. Ideologically, he was in favour of developing Turkey's ties with the western democracies, in line with the final objective of establishing political democracy in Turkey. This ideological inclination towards a western alliance was also strengthened by geo-political and strategic considerations. As mentioned above, the most immediate and gravest dangers threatening Turkish security during the 1930s were Italian and especially German expansionism. With Russia, the Treaty of Friendship signed in Moscow in 1925 between Turkey and the Soviet Union remained in force. However, on historical, geo-political and ideological ground, question marks about Russian intentions seemed bound to come up, especially after the Soviet Union had regained enough military and economic strength. Atatürk's move towards better relations with Britain could not long remain unnoticed in Moscow. The shift in Turkish foreign policy, whatever its purpose, was bound to raise questions in the Soviet Union.

In fact, as has been described in a recent article by Ambassador İsmail Soysal and published in the Bulletin of the Turkish Historical Society, the attitude of the Soviet Union towards

Turkey underwent a marked change in the years 1935 and 1936.[5] The change occurred after the Turkish Government approached the Soviet Government in 1935, through the Turkish Ambassador in Moscow, Zekai Apaydın, with a proposal for the signature of a treaty of mutual assistance in the case of an Italian aggression against Turkey. The Soviet Government, arguing that such a pact would unnecessarily arouse suspicions in Italy and in Germany, rejected the Turkish proposal. Subsequently, in June 1936, just after the opening of the Montreux conference on the Straits, the Soviet Foreign Minister Litvinoff suggested to his Turkish colleague, Rüstü Aras, a treaty of alliance between Turkey and the Soviet Union, with the object of the joint defence of the Straits. Litvinoff added that the Soviet Union would assist Turkey in the building of fortifications in the Straits. He finally suggested that Turkey send a written note to the Soviet Government requesting this aid.

The Russian proposal was met with incomprehension and misgiving in Ankara. After some further exchange of views between Russian and Turkish diplomats over the subject, the Turkish Government replied in October 1936 to the Soviet Government through the Turkish Ambassador in Moscow. The content and tone of this reply had been determined by the Turkish Cabinet and approved by Atatürk.[6] The reply dismissed the idea of submitting any Turkish written proposal to the Soviets about the joint defence of the Straits, but reiterated Turkish goodwill and friendship towards the Soviet Union. It appears that the Turkish Foreign Minister had secretly informed the British Foreign Secretary Anthony Eden of the Soviet request in October 1936, in Geneva, and had asked his view on the matter.[7] The official British reply was handed soon after to Fethi Okyar. The British note stated that the Russian proposal would involve a military alliance between Turkey and Russia, and therefore would end by tying Turkey to one of the blocs then emerging in Europe. The British said that Turkey's strength came from its neutral position in the Mediterranean, from which it was able to exercise its influence towards peace and stability. Therefore, to ensure its own security, it was preferable that Turkey should not tie itself to one bloc.

The above developments in Turco-Soviet relations should be seen in the light of the marked shift in Turkish foreign policy in the early 1930s, towards friendship and co-operation with Western European states and above all with Britain. The main factors behind this shift were, as noted, geo-political and strategic. The need to seek greater security in the face of growing German and Italian expansionism was the dominating element which brought Turkey and Britain together at the end of the thirties. At the same time, Turkey's growing ties with the West affected her relations with Soviet Russia. The latter was trying to avoid taking sides as between the western and the Axis powers. She would have liked to reassume the traditional Russian objectives, and to strengthen her leverage over both European blocs, through a military alliance with Turkey, involving joint control of the Straits.

The complementary shifts in Turkish and in British foreign policies were certainly helped by the activities of diplomats such as Fethi Okyar and Percy Loraine. The story of Percy Loraine's activities and of his role in bringing together Britain and Turkey has already been told.[8] The purpose of this paper has been to throw some light on the role and activities of Fethi Okyar during his second mission as Atatürk's representative in London. The outcome of this second mission in 1939 marked a complete turn around in British-Turkish relations, from the depths to which they had sunk after the First World War.

NOTES

1. Yusuf Kemal Tengirşenk, *Vatan Hizmetinde* (Istanbul, 1967).
2. Cemal Kutay, *Üç Devirde Bir Adam: Fethi Okyar* (Istanbul, 1980).
3. Philip Graves, *Briton and Turk* (London, 1941) p. 227 ff.
4. Gordon Waterfield, *Professional Diplomat: Sir Percy Loraine* (London, 1973) p. 209.
5. İsmail Soysal 'Türkiye'nin Batı İttifakına Yöneliği', *Tarih Kurumu Belleteni*, vol. 45, no. 177 (Jan. 1981).
6. See ibid.
7. Ibid., p. 136.
8. Waterfield, op. cit.

VII

TURCO-BRITISH RELATIONS SINCE THE 1920S

Ömer Kürkçüoğlu

Turco-British relations, after experiencing only one period of direct belligerency between 1914 to 1918, began to be increasingly close from the 1920s onwards. First there was a period of indirect war but later on closer relations were established that eventually led to an alliance, once thorny problems between the two sides had been resolved. How was this achieved?

In this paper I shall examine this process in its various phases. In the conclusion I shall try to point out certain fundamental trends in Turco-British relations.

I RELATIONS IN THE 1920s

(i) Until 1926

The question of peace with Turkey was the remaining issue for Britain and her allies after the Ottoman Empire signed the Mudros Armistice on 30 October 1918. Until the last quarter of the nineteenth century, Britain had pursued a policy of protecting the territorial integrity of the Ottoman Empire: however, after 1878, and particularly after the Ottoman Empire entered the First World War on the side of Germany, Britain adopted a policy aimed at dismembering the Empire. There was strong competition between Britain and her allies for the Ottoman territories. Agreements were signed between Britain, France, Russia and Italy during the First World War. In spite of various inter-allied disputes concerning these agreements, all the allies – except Russia, which was separated from the Entente by the 1917 Revolution – began to reorganise the territories of the Ottoman Empire within the framework of their agreements after the war.

Britain was in a very powerful position after the war. However, there were important disputes between the allies as well as new problems arising with Britain itself and in her Empire. Due to these difficulties Britain was anxious to make peace and to avoid the danger of entering a new war. Apart from having a partial say as regards the future of the Arab territories, Britain was anxious to establish an Armenian and/or a Kurdish state in the north of Mesopotamia as a barrier against Soviet Russia and also to rely on an enlarged Greece in Western Anatolia. A reduced Ottoman Sultanate would be allowed to survive in Istanbul. Since early 1918, when the Union and Progress leaders left the country, the new Ottoman administration was friendly towards Britain. Britain could therefore rely on the friendship of the Ottomans. Amity with the Caliph would be beneficial for Britain, particularly in the context of Indian politics, since she had 'the greatest Moslem population'. Having thus gained an influence at the Straits, Britain would have achieved yet another bulwark against Soviet Russia.

Such a policy seemed quite natural from the viewpoint of British interests. However the rise of the nationalist movement in Anatolia under the leadership of Atatürk after May 1919 placed this policy in jeopardy. The conflict was to continue until the British recognised the strength of the nationalist movement in Anatolia, and turned towards a policy of relying on a new and powerful Turkish state.

There was thus a period of indirect war between Britain and the National Government in Ankara between 1919 and 1923. In fact, pending the signing of a peace treaty between Britain and the Ottoman Empire, a direct state of war continued to exist *de jure*. Although the Treaty of Sèvres was signed with the Ottoman Government on 10 August 1920 this Treaty did not come into force – not only because it remained unratified by both the Ottoman Government and other countries but also because it was rejected by the nationalists in Anatolia.

Under these circumstances a state of war between Turkey, Britain and her allies continued to exist.

During the war in Anatolia an indirect state of war existed between the British forces and the nationalists, although there were also at times direct skirmishes between the British and Turks. The nationalists were in fact fighting indirectly against Britain and her allies in the course of the struggle against invading Greek forces. The war of liberation was a remorseless struggle conducted in both the military and diplomatic fields. It was a war with many facets which was waged against both internal enemies (in the shape of the Sultan's Government in Istanbul) and also against foreign occupation. Atatürk followed external events closely: he foresaw the future clearly in the light of the lessons he had learnt from past history and understood the nature of the disputes between the great powers. He attached great importance to leaving open the option of dialogue with the enemy. The nationalist movement used the aid which it received from the Islamic world and from Soviet Russia cautiously and was not dragged into adventurism. It followed a cautious policy towards the Soviet régime. In spite of this attitude, Britain saw the nationalist movement as a pro-Soviet one. At the outset the British did not properly appreciate the limits of the relationship between the nationalist government in Ankara and the Soviet regime. However the demonstration of the military strength of the nationalist movement after 1921, and the realisation that nationalist Turkey did not follow a Soviet model mitigated the attitude of the British, so that they began a dialogue with the Ankara government.

However, this process went through some serious ups and downs. The feeling that there was almost a state of war between the two countries, which had developed in the autumn of 1922, continued until the signing of the Mudanya Armistice on 11 October 1922. The Lausanne peace conference, which began on 20 November 1922, adjourned on 4 February 1923 and re-opened on 23 April 1923. It was concluded with the signature of the peace treaty of 24 July 1923. During the Lausanne negotiations, a bitter struggle developed between Britain and her allies on the one hand and the National Turkish Government on the other. However, this confrontation heralded a period of co-operation during the following period. Atatürk had learnt the lesson of Ottoman history and was planning to establish a new Turkish state in a contemporary westernised and Europeanised mould. Even during the war of liberation, he had made his views clear: he was waging a war against the West for the sake of westernisation.

During the Lausanne talks the British became aware of the fact that it would be to their advantage to turn towards a re-established Turkish state especially as an obstacle to Russian advances. Such a state could be accepted as a member of the European comity of nations in sharp contrast to its Ottoman predecessors. For her part, Turkey had demonstrated her power to the British, and was in a position to re-create friendly relations with them. In addition, Atatürk was concerned about the position of the Soviet Union, with which he had collaborated during the war of liberation. For this reason, while maintaining a certain degree of friendship with Russia, he was anxious to balance Turco-Soviet relations with links with the West – and especially with Britain which was seen as the most powerful of the western countries.

The Turkish attitude towards their relations with the outside world and Britain after the war of liberation was as follows. After the signature of the Treaty of Lausanne, Turkey was preoccupied with domestic affairs and was determined to cure her backwardness by means of a rapid orientation towards Western values. However certain problems remained in foreign policy, which proved to be of continuing concern to Turkey. There were some unresolved points left over from the Treaty of Lausanne which remained a problem for Turkey until the beginning of the 1930s. The Mosul dispute, which concerned the British mandate administration in Iraq, was probably the most important of the points of dispute between Turkey and Britain. At the time of the signature of the Mudros armistice of 30 October 1918 Mosul was still under the control of Ottoman forces and was considered to be inside the boundaries of the future Turkish state which was envisaged in the National Pact. A few days later, however, the British occupied the region, after bringing pressure to bear on the Sixth Army Commander, General Ali İhsan.

Mosul proved a controversial issue during the Lausanne negotiations but no lasting solution to this dispute was reached. Turkey was in favour of a plebiscite on this question which would define the final boundaries between Turkey and Iraq but the British rejected this proposal. The Turks, who noticed that the British were quite sensitive on the questions of the Straits and Mosul, favoured a common resolution of the first problem which proved to be to their advantage: however, the second problem was left unresolved. Article 3 of the Lausanne Treaty envisaged that if the parties failed to find a solution within nine months, the issue would be referred to the League of Nations. A solution could not be achieved, however, although talks between the two parties lasted from 5 October 1923 to June 1924. In the end the issue was submitted to the League of Nations on 20 September 1924.

The two countries, who had experienced a state of indirect war during the War of Independence, now faced a new and direct confrontation. At that time Turkey was not a member of the League of Nations, in which Britain was the dominating power. The League of Nations resolution of 16 December 1925 on the Mosul dispute favoured the British case, but created a severe crisis in Turco-British relations. In this climate, relations between Turkey and the Soviet Union were revitalised. The Soviet Union was not a member of the League of Nations either and expected to gain advantage from closer ties with Turkey, since she felt that the Locarno Agreements signed between Germany and the West were aimed at her.

Although Turkey seriously contemplated the possibility of war, she could not risk renewed fighting only four years after the War of Independence – particularly against a country such as Britain, which was one of the world's major powers at the time. Such a risk would endanger the peace which Turkey needed for her rapid development. Turkey believed that Britain could well go to war over the Mosul dispute,[1] since it was of vital importance for her interests. She therefore was obliged to abandon this particular objective of the National Pact, and remained loyal to the fundamental features of Atatürk's foreign policy – realism and non adventurism. With the Agreement on Borders and Good Neighbourliness which was signed in Ankara on 5 June 1926 with the Governments of Britain and Iraq, Turkey accepted the League of Nations decision on Mosul – namely to cede Mosul to Iraq, which was then under British mandate administration.

(ii) After 1926

Following the resolution of the Mosul dispute in 1926 relations between Britain and Turkey entered a period of stagnation. The elimination of the fundamental problem between the two countries formed a foundation for an improved relationship. Nevertheless, because the Mosul dispute had dragged the two sides to the brink of war, the establishment of close relations was neither easy nor rapid. The Locarno Agreements created a climate of relative peace – a 'golden age' in inter-war history – during the second half of the 1920s. This was a period in which Britain concentrated upon domestic issues and developments in Europe, whereas Turkey moved towards a solution of some of the less important problems left over from the Lausanne Treaty and towards rapid domestic modernisation.

It was in this period that the move of the British Embassy from Istanbul to Ankara took place. Delay in moving their embassies from the ancient capital of Istanbul to Ankara by the great powers, and particularly by the British, can be traced to the political antagonisms which were rooted in the War of Independence, although British officials also mentioned the difficult living conditions in Ankara and the fact that none of the British diplomats could be forced to settle there.[2] The resolution of this problem eliminated one of the factors which threatened relations between Britain and Turkey.

During this period, Turco-British relations were at times close but also went through some difficult periods. Some documents from this period demonstrate these ups and downs. In an interview published in *Stamboul* of 5 and 6 February 1927, the Minister of Foreign Affairs, Tevfik Rüstü Aras, stated '[Relations with Britain] . . . have become friendly since the Iraq treaty was signed . . . Turkey sacrificed Mosul in the higher interest of peace'.[3] On the other hand, in his confidential report from Istanbul dated 30 March 1927, Mr Hoare stated that Ghazi Mustafa Kemal, during a ball in Ankara, indicated his uneasiness regarding the anti-Turkish activities in Britain of certain Jews – who, the Ghazi said, were a menace to Turkey – and by Turkish political refugees such as Halide Edip. Mr Hoare added that 'the Ghazi hinted that he intended to publish certain correspondence which would lead HMG to take action against them'.[4]

During this period the visit of the British fleet caused the reappearance of traces of hostility in relations between Turkey and Britain. In his reports from Istanbul dated 7 and 11 May 1927 Sir George Clerk gave information about the summer programme of the Mediterranean Fleet.[5] He said 'The Ministry of Foreign Affairs states that the Turkish Government would be very happy to receive a courtesy visit of a *passing* British squadron but a special visit would amount to demonstration of relations which did not exist. If part of Fleet is going to Black Sea, visit can be arranged on its way up. Presumes that it would be "informal"'. It appears that at the same time Britain doubted whether Mustafa Kemal could retain his post. In his letter to Mr Oliphant, dated 15 June 1927, Clerk stated that 'two German doctors who examined Mr Kemal are said to have given "no hope", and there is talk of Kazim Karabekir'. However, Clerk was 'doubtful as to early crisis'.[6]

A little later a more optimistic atmosphere in Turco-British relations was to re-emerge. In his statement of 16 February 1928, given to *The Times*' correspondent, J.W. Collins, the Minister of Foreign Affairs, Tevfik Rüstü Aras, said 'Our relations with Iraq and Britain are excellent . . . When I signed the Iraq Treaty 20 months ago I never dreamed that our relations would be as good as they are now'.[7] In this atmosphere the visit of a British fleet to Istanbul revitalised Turco-

British relations and heralded a further *rapprochement* in the future. When one considers the difficulties faced by such a visit only two years before, which we have noted already, its significance becomes still greater.

The visit of the British Mediterranean Fleet, which took place in October 1929, and Admiral Field's visit to Ankara for talks with Mustafa Kemal and high-level officials were received positively in the Turkish press, as British officials noted. In his report from Istanbul of 23 October 1929, Clerk remarked 'Most important article was by Necmeddin Sadak in *Akşam*, which at no time can be accused of pro-British tendencies; tone of article was friendly and Sadak Bey greeted visit as a happy preface to new era of close relations between Great Britain and Turkey'.[8] Sadak had added that Admiral Field's journey to Ankara 'increased the importance of the visit', that 'nations had to forget the past for peace', and that 'after periods of trouble and stress, friendship becomes easier and more sincere'. In a Foreign Office note of 7 October 1929, the front page cartoon of the magazine *Köroğlu* dated 28 September 1929 was put forward as 'remarkable indication of revulsion of Turkish public opinion in favour of Great Britain'.[9] The cartoon showed a typical middle-aged Anatolian Turk, complete with cloth cap, standing near the sea and hoisting the Turkish flag to the mast while looking towards the British ships which loomed ahead. The caption read 'the Turkish nation, which protected its national home with the breasts of its sons, opens its door with delight to friends. Come along, gentlemen!'

II RELATIONS IN THE 1930s

During the early 1930s Turkey, having solved the problems remaining from Lausanne and achieved internal reforms, was ready to deal with international problems with greater confidence. In the second half of the 1920s, a period in which she was dealing with both domestic and foreign problems, she was interested in international co-operation. The new Turkish state was ready to take its share of responsibility for world peace, in line with Atatürk's principle of 'peace at home, peace in the world' and the humanitarian values which went with it. As an example she was immediately attracted to the Briand-Kellogg Pact signed on 27 August 1928 and indicated her wish to take part: she acceeded to the Pact in January 1929. During the early 1930s Turkey was able to fulfill her international responsibilities more easily. At this date international relations were deteriorating and a period of further crisis was developing. The close co-operation established between the Foreign Ministers of Britain, France and Germany (Chamberlain, Briand and Stresemann) ended both because they left office and as a result of the economic crisis of 1929–30. Disputes over the reorganisation of post-1918 Europe began to come to the surface again. The division between the revisionist and anti-revisionist states was emerging.

In this framework Turkey, as the country which had signed the Lausanne Treaty, the only post-war agreement which depended on mutual negotiation, and which had largely achieved the goals of the War of Liberation, was clearly disinclined to participate in the revisionist front – in spite of the fact that she believed that certain unjust measures had been taken against Germany in the Versailles Treaty and that the National Pact contained certain goals which were still unrealised. As the basic premiss of Atatürk's foreign policy was 'to keep the gates of dialogue open even with the enemy', she continued her relations with the revisionist states.[10] Moreover, as Italy became an increasing threat in the Eastern Mediterranean, (and from time to time an open threat to Turkey), Turkey for her part became increasingly anxious about the objectives of the revisionist states as the years went by. She did not want to be dragged into the war and, although not over-worried by the possibility of an attack by Italy,[11] she was nevertheless concerned that such an attack might develop. Since Turkey was basically committed to peace, the Italian factor together with the favourable climate maintained in relations with Britain during the early 1930s, led Turkey towards closer co-operation with Britain and France. At the same time the Soviet Union, as a neighbour with whom Turkey had always sought to maintain fairly close relations, moved towards a better relationship with the British and French. This made Turkey's task easier. Apart from this, the resolution of controversial issues between Turkey and Greece, created a positive attitude in Britain towards Turkey.[12] The parallel flow of interest between Turkey and Britain at this time had both indirect and direct aspects, which will be examined later. Indirect co-operation took three forms: entry to the League of Nations, leadership in the Balkan Entente and leadership in the Sadabad Pact.

Turkey faced many difficulties due to her non-membership of the League of Nations, especially during the Mosul dispute. Turkey's interest in joining the League of Nations, which was under the domination of the victors of the First World War, increased when her relations with these countries improved. Turkey became a member of the League of Nations in 1932 when her relations with the West – particularly with Britain – reached a turning point: the same was true of Germany, as her relations with the western powers improved after the Locarno Agreements of 1925. Thus, in a period when post-war reorganisation faced major challenges, Turkey established indirect co-operation with the democratic states, and with Britain in particular.[13] This co-operation was effective in the solution of the Straits problem, which was achieved at Montreux in 1936.[14]

Italy, as one of the revisionist states, directed her attention towards the Balkans and the Eastern Mediterranean and was thus a source of discomfort for Turkey, the other countries of the region and Britain. A new step was taken with the signature of the Balkan Entente on 9 February 1934, under the leadership of Turkey and Greece with the participation of Romania and Yugoslavia. The latter two states were the allies of the French in the little Entente. In this way an indirect alliance was created between Britain and France. Turkey had thus taken a step towards indirect co-operation with the British and French.

Turkey also took the lead in the conclusion of the Sadabad Pact on 8 July 1937 with Iran, Iraq and Afghanistan. This pact created a new chain of indirect co-operation between Britain and Turkey, since Britain was involved as the mandatory power in Iraq. The Italian attack on Ethiopia of 1935 caused concern on the part of both Britain and Turkey.

The indirect co-operation between Turkey and Britain opened the way for direct collaboration between the two countries. The two developments emerging during this period were, on the one hand, the promotion of economic co-operation and, on the other, a mutual alliance. The Turkish Foreign Minister, Tevfik Rüstü Aras, told the British Ambassador in December 1932 that a non-aggression pact was being considered between Turkey, Iran and Iraq and that 'it was hoped that Britain would accede'.[15] Mr Ramsay, in his secret report from Athens of 14 October 1933, said that he 'learned from reliable source that M. Venizelos remarked, while giving an account of his recent visit to [Turkey] to one of his most trusted partisans, that M. Kemal had stated that Turkey would do her best not to go to war but, if she did, it would be on side which held command of sea'.[16] The British Ambassador to Ankara, Sir Percy Loraine, in a confidential report from Istanbul of 22 June 1934, said that the fact that the new Turkish Ambassador in London, Fethi Bey, was Atatürk's close friend, showed that Atatürk believed Turco-British friendship was not only 'desirable' but also 'possible'.[17]

Sir Percy presented his views on the evolution of Turkish foreign policy in a despatch of 7 July 1934.[18] He remarked that Turkey's foreign policy was now closer to that of her former enemies than to that of her former friends. Sir Percy added:

> Turkey is actually anti-revisionist; is pro-League of Nations: is content with her own frontiers: is hostile to the splitting up of powers into opposite camps or blocs: is an advocate of international cooperation; works for the reduction of international frictions . . .[19]

At this point the Italian problem was coming to the surface: on the Ethiopia issue Turkey and Britain were in direct co-operation within the framework of the Mediterranean Pact.[20] In the meantime, Turkey proposed a treaty of alliance to Britain;[21] however this was not achieved since Britain did not regard this proposal as suiting her policy.[22] Nevertheless, the *rapprochment* between the two countries continued to develop towards an alliance: in a report of 1 December 1936 to Mr Rendel, Sir Percy Loraine gave information about King Edward VIII's visit to Istanbul and said that the King's visit aroused affection not only at the governmental level but also among the people.[23] In a further despatch dated 9 April 1937 to the Secretary of State,[24] Loraine reported a statement made by the Turkish Foreign Minister, Mr Aras, to the effect that: 'Turkey had definitely linked her destinies to the United Kingdom'. The Turkish Foreign Minister had remarked that Turkey did this willingly, confidently and totally. He added that Turkey had two great friendships: one of them was with Russia. This was 'firm and indestructible, but limited strictly to the written engagements we have accepted and are public'. The other one, with Britain 'is actually an alliance, and is unlimited'. Aras added that there was nothing in written form between Turkey and Britain but that there was mutual friendship and trust which were more important.

A little later, the trends which led to an alliance between the two countries gained momentum. Despite the 'pacification policy' of Britain, Germany's *fait accompli* ended in the occupation of Czechoslovakia on 15 March 1939; this led Britain to take counter-measures. Britain and France wanted to guarantee Greece, Romania and Turkey against attack; however, Turkey proposed that this collaboration should take the form of an alliance. The meetings between Britain, France[25] and Turkey ended with the Turco-British and Turco-French Declarations of 12 May 1939 and 23 June 1939 respectively. These documents indicated how well advanced the preparations that led to the Turco-British-French alliance were at this stage.[26]

As already mentioned, Turkey, while promoting her relations with the West during the 1930s, considered that the recovery of her relations with the West and the Soviet Union (with whom she was anxious not to reduce relations below a certain level) as a positive step. However, she was left in a difficult situation when the Soviet Union signed a Non-aggression Pact with Nazi Germany on 23 August 1939. Although the text of the Turco-British-French alliance had already been prepared, the Turkish Foreign Minister went to Moscow on 24 September 1939 to establish whether it would be possible to maintain Soviet friendship together with this alliance. However, when this visit made it clear that it was impossible to put off further the alliance with Britain and France, the Turco-British-French Pact was signed on 19 October, while the Foreign Minister, Mr Saraçoğlu was on his way back from Moscow.

When the British Prime Minister, Neville Chamberlain, told the House of Commons on 19 October 1939 'I am glad to be able to announce to the House that the [Turco-French-British] Treaty was signed at Angora half an hour ago',[27] Mr Attlee shared the same pleasure and expressed his hope for the future: '[I] hope that it may long endure and that our friendship with Turkey may be strengthened for many years to come'. Sir Percy Harris, also, congratulated the Government upon 'this great victory' and said: ' . . . Turkey has been one of the countries that has made immense progress in the arts of civilisation and economic development and therefore it is very satisfactory to us that they should be standing alongside this country . . . '

III THE SECOND WORLD WAR

Turkey, taking account of her experiences during the First World War, was determined not to take part in the Second unless she were attacked and were fully prepared for war. During the first phase of the war (1939–1941) Germany enjoyed definite superiority. In 1940, the attacks of Italy first on France and then on Greece constituted sufficient reason for Turkey to join the war: however she stayed out of it by implementing the second protocol of the Pact – the requirement that stated that if Turkey's guarantees arising from the Pact caused a Turco-Soviet war, then it would be invalid. Turkey believed that she was not fully prepared. During this period, Germany could easily have excluded Turkey from the fighting: this would have created a danger for Britain in the Middle East. Therefore, Britain reacted to Turkey's failure to enter the war with understanding. Moreover, Turkey refused to give Germany permission to cross Turkey to support the pro-German uprising of Rashid Ali al-Geylani in Iraq in 1941, and thus made it possible for Britain to suppress the revolt. Thus, during the first phase of the war, Turkey's relations with Britain continued in a framework of co-operation although Turkey did not actually participate in the war.

The second phase (1941–1943) was one in which the belligerent parties were more evenly balanced. The allied countries gradually increased the pressure on Turkey with a view to securing her participation in the war. Nevertheless Britain understood Turkey's need for preparation, and in this way contacts between the two countries were carried forward. Granted this atmosphere, the meetings in Adana between the British Prime Minister Winston Churchill and the President of Turkey İsmet İnönü, which were held on 30 January – 1 February 1943, took place in a spirit of mutual understanding and co-operation.[28]

During the final phase of the war (1943–1945) it became obvious that pressure on Turkey to join the war increased. To complete the defeat of Germany as soon as possible, Turkey's entry into the war would have been helpful to the allied cause: for example, had planes been able to use bases in Turkey this would have helped to end German superiority in the Aegean. According to the Allies, Turkey's demands would have taken so long to meet that the war would have been over by the time they were fulfilled.[29] It should be remembered, however, that Turkey had not forgotten the bitter experiences of the First World War. The fact that the Soviet Union was also insisting on Turkish participation was very disturbing for the Turks. Turkey did not want to be occupied by Germany only to be 'liberated' by the Soviet Union at the end of the war. From early 1944 a crisis of confidence developed between Turkey and Britain. Britain and the United States stopped military aid to Turkey, and even ceased passing on information about the war to the Turks.[30] Although Turkey declared war on the common enemy on 23 February 1945, the dispute between the Allies and Turkey was not resolved. Essentially, Turkey's decision was made to fulfill the pledge taken at the Yalta conference to qualify her for founding membership of the United Nations.

IV THE POST-1945 PERIOD

Deserted by her allies, Turkey came under increasing pressure from the Soviet Union after March 1945. The USSR announced that the 1925 Treaty of Friendship and Non-aggression would not be renewed. When Turkey asked the Soviet Union what would be her conditions for renewal of the Treaty the Soviets began to put heavy pressure on Turkey. This pressure took the form of several different demands.

Faced with this dangerous security threat, Turkey made various approaches to Britain and the United States. However at this stage the co-operation which had begun during the war between the West and the Soviet Union was still continuing. As an example, British officials remarked that 'Turkey would not be facing such a situation if she had entered the war'.[31] Britain, and particularly the United States, were of the opinion that the Soviet Union would not attack Turkey, thanks to the structures that were being established within the framework of the United Nations.

Throughout 1945 Turkey went through a very difficult period. Until the end of the year the non-aggression guarantee which was contained in the 1925 Treaty with the Soviet Union was still in force. Nevertheless, Turkey was prepared for a possible attack. At the same time, certain issues were in dispute between the West and the Soviet Union. The cooling of relations between the two sides opened the way for greater western concern for Turkey's complaints. When the Soviet Union submitted a note to Turkey concerning the Straits in August 1946, Turkey received the support of both the Americans and the British. The exchange of notes which took place showed that there was clear co-operation between Turkey, the USA and Britain.[32] During the post-1945 period, the UA's leadership of the western bloc clearly emerged.

Thanks to the increasing burdens which were being placed on her in the Balkans (such as the civil war in Greece) and especially in the Middle East, (such as the Palestine problem), Britain asked the United States to take her share of the defence burden.

This situation was of considerable importance for the development of Anglo-Turkish relations. In the post-war world Turkey was drawing closer to the West, thus reinforcing a development which had begun in the 1930s, but her relationship with the United States represented the centre of gravity of her relations with the Western Powers generally. During this period, although the military and political presence of Britain in the Middle East continued, there was some evidence of British withdrawal from the region; under these circumstances, Turco-American relations took precedence over Turco-British relations.

In the early 1950s, Turkey's basic goal was to join the western alliance, and in particular to take part in NATO, which had been established in 1949. However, at the outset, Britain wanted Turkey to join a regional pact, or joint command in the Middle East, rather than take part in NATO, and even suggested that Turkey should lead such an organisation. Turkey, with NATO membership as her main goal, saw no harm in playing an active role in the Middle East. She joined Britain and France in the proposal that Egypt should support the proposed Middle East Command. The Egyptians, however, rejected this proposal and the project came to nought. In this way the final obstacle to Turkey's membership of NATO was eliminated. NATO approved the membership of Turkey on 16 to 20 September 1951 and made a formal announcement to this effect on 18 February 1952.

With her entry into NATO Turkey was once more allied with Britain. This led to closer relations between the two countries which have continued to develop since then. Apart from this, however, Turkey's relations with Britain have been affected by two other important problems – in the Middle East and in Cyprus. These will each be considered in turn.

The mid-1950s was a period of tension in the Middle East

since the Cold War was emerging in Europe at this time. Turkey was playing a leading role in the Baghdad Pact, which had been established on 24 February 1955. Britain joined the Pact organisation on 4 April 1955. The Baghdad Pact represented a new framework for collaboration between the two countries. However, Britain's attack on Suez of 30 October 1956 occasioned a strong reaction in the Arab world. Turkey demonstrated a guarded response to the attack thanks to her membership of the Baghdad Pact. Turkey had her own reasons for improving her relations with the West. At the same time the Arab states' relations with the Western Powers were cooling – again, for their own reasons – and the path followed by Turkey then diverged from that of her Arab neighbours. In fact, Turkey failed to understand how the Arab world could fail to feel the same sensitivity against the Soviet Union which she felt herself.

The Baghdad Pact, which provoked unfavourable reactions on the part of the Arab countries and gave Turkey a negative image in the region, was renamed CENTO in 1959 after the withdrawal of its only Arab member, Iraq. It was formally abolished in 1979.

In the post-war period, Greece took note of the fact that Britain was withdrawing from her colonies and from the Middle East in general. The Greeks believed that the principle of self-determination should apply to Cyprus and referred the matter to the United Nations. The emergence of the Cyprus dispute after 1954 constituted a problem which affected Turkey, Greece and Britain – all members of NATO.

At the outset, Turkey, in the belief that this question should not create a problem between the Allies, supported the continuation of a British administration in Cyprus. However, as the demands for British withdrawal increased, Turkey proposed that she should be included in future discussions about the island. The period 1955 to 1959 was overshadowed by terrorist activities on the part of the Greek Cypriots, and by British attempts to find a solution to the problem. In the end, as a result of meetings held in Zurich and London in 1959, a consensus was reached between Britain, Turkey, Greece and the Greek and Turkish Cypriots. The new arrangement, while giving Cyprus her independence, provided for British bases on the island, and set out the position of the two communities in the framework of a republican constitution. In the event of the collapse of these arrangements which were provided in the constitution, Greece and Britain retained the right to intervene multilaterally or unilaterally.

After a relatively peaceful period between 1960 and 1963, Turco-British co-operation on the Cyprus question went through a critical phase during the latter part of 1963. At the time of the pro-Greek *coup d'état* of 15 July 1974, Turkey attempted to confer on the question of intervention with the British. However, the Turkish and British Governments failed to reach a consensus during the meetings which were held in London that summer. Accordingly, Turkey intervened unilaterally in Cyprus on 20 July 1974. No solution to the Cyprus problem has been found since then. Gradually, Turco-British relations have become less affected by this problem. As British presence in the Middle East, and thus her influence in the Cyprus question, has decreased, so the obstacles in the path of Turco-British relations have been gradually eliminated.

Turco-British relations over the last sixty years has seen a shift from friendship to rivalry and back to friendship.[33] Today, however, the relations between the two countries are founded on a stronger basis. It is very clear that if Turkey remains strong and co-operates with Britain against the common danger, and retains her western-orientated political structure without threatening British economic and political interests in the Middle East, Britain's need for co-operation with Turkey will continue. As has been explained already, the need for mutual friendship between the two countries became clearer during the Republican period. Atatürk, who had encountered soldiers of many nations, both large and small, in the battlefield, had reached some very sound conclusions about them. Among them, the British occupied a special place. Atatürk had deep feelings of understanding and respect towards them. The fact that he pressed for friendship with the

British, whom he found to be a noble people, even at a time of enmity, arose from this.[34]

It also seems clear that the British have shared these feelings. The respect felt by the British fighting the Turks at the Dardanelles was demonstrated in many books written on the subject. As an expression of this feeling 'The Clean Fighting Turk' became the headline for many articles printed during the First World War and later. The majority of the MPs who delivered pro-Turkish speeches during the War of Independence in the British Parliament were of military origin and had fought against the Turks in the Dardanelles. Those who were strongly anti-Turkish were mainly those who knew little of the Turks, whereas those who were strongly pro-Turkish had close acquaintance with the Turks and who fought against them. Both nations were 'a noble enemy and a great friend' to each other. There are many similarities between the two countries.[35] Common characteristics include reticence,[36] patience, loyalty, discipline and a spirit of national solidarity; as individuals, the two peoples may seem introverted, but the closest of friendships can develop once the ice has been broken.

NOTES

1. Lord Kinross (author of *Atatürk: a biography of Mustafa Kemal, Father of Modern Turkey*, W. Morrow, New York, 1965) said to me during an interview on 16 January 1974 that Britain could never have gone to war for the sake of Mosul and that it would have given way if Turkey had insisted more stubbornly. Lord Kinross argued that to cede Mosul to Iraq 'was Atatürk's sole mistake in foreign policy'. He went on to say that at the time Britain was anxious to seek solutions to mutual problems and that she would not have insisted on Mosul. 'Moreover', he added, 'Britain was not aware of the value of Mosul's oil'. According to Lord Kinross 'Turkey, too, was not aware of the oil'; if Turkey had been aware of it and insisted on her claim Britain would have given way. Lord Kinross attributed Atatürk's non-insistence to – among other factors – 'the importance he had attached to British friendship since Gallipoli'. However, I would suggest that when looked at from the Turkish viewpoint at the time it appeared that Britain would go to war. As I have explained, Turkey could not accept such a serious risk.
2. British Foreign Minister Austen Chamberlain in a despatch to the representative in Paris, Lord Crewe, said that HMG could not ask a

diplomat of ambassadorial rank '... to submit to the conditions of residence in a dirty little mountain village in the centre of Anatolia' or 'condemn [him] to a painful and inglorious exile in the latter town'. Chamberlain added that such a diplomat 'ought not be exiled to the squalor and fleas of Angora as his permanent residence' and concluded 'Since Turkey remains in Europe, let us get what little advantage we can out of her presence here'. FO 371/10194; E9848/210/44.
The Lord Privy Seal (The Marquess of Salisbury), in his speech to the House of Lords on 2 February 1926, attributed the fact that the British Embassy had not been transferred to Ankara to the accommodation being 'rather primitive' there. He added: 'At any rate, I share ... the hope that before very long there will be some possibility of a permanent residence at Angora. At present it is not possible. We are doing all we can do to renew the full friendly relations with Turkey ...' HL (House of Lords), Deb. 5s., p. 27. Viscount Haldane, who spoke earlier (p. 19) said that the transfer of the Embassy to Ankara was necessary although it was expensive, since 'the Ambassador had to be there'. Viscount Haldane added: 'You cannot settle ... things in the East without a great deal of conversation and personal communication. Indeed, it is on personal communication that one most depends, and we have had lessons in recent time of how much we have suffered in this country from not thoroughly understanding the affairs of the Near East'.

3. FO 371/12308; E746/17/44.
4. FO 371/12308; E1575/17/44.
5. FO 371/12653; W4592/3953/50.
6. FO 371/12320; E2885/257/44.
7. From Sir G. Clerk to Mr. Oliphant, Private and Confidential, 23 February 1928; FO 371/13085; E124/43/44.
8. FO 371/13828; E5545/5419/44.
9. FO 371/13812; E5163/92/44.
10. A statement by the Foreign Minister T.R. Aras of 27 November 1933 described Turkey as 'anti-revisionist'. In another statement in 1934, T.R. Aras said Turkey was '*a-revisioniste*' (non-revisionist). Edward Weisband, *The Sanajak of Alexandretta 1920–1939: a case study* (prepared for the Near Eastern Round Table of 10 May 1968, Center for International Studies) p. 10 and Aptülahat Akşin, *Atatürk'ün Dış Politika İlkeleri ve Diplomasisi*, (İkinci Kısım, Istanbul, 1966) p. 147.
11. According to the British Ambassador in Ankara Sir Hugh Knatchbull-Hugessen's despatch to Lord Halifax, dated 28 April 1939, Turkish Foreign Minister Aras told the German Ambassador von Papen: 'the Turks do not fear the Italians. Our superiority over them is that they are Italians and we are Turks'. Erol Ulubelen (ed.), *İngiliz Gizli Belgelerinde Türkiye* (Istanbul, 1967) pp. 298–9.
12. Philip P. Graves, *Briton and Turk*, (London, 1941) p. 225.

13. The fact that Turkey tried to make the transition to multi-party democracy at the beginning of the 1930s, when she was also working for good relations with the Western countries is an interesting coincidence. Although the Free Party experiment in 1930 was of short duration, the single-party regime in Turkey was, nevertheless, different from other single-party regimes in Europe: indeed, the Turkish regime felt itself to be closer to the liberal democracies. In experimenting with multi-party rule, Atatürk was influenced by the British model: Hikmet Bil, *Atatürk'ün Sofrasında*, (n.p., n.d.) pp. 54–6.
14. Foreign Minister T.R. Aras, mentions the understanding and interest in this affair of 'his friend' Anthony Eden. Tevfik Rüstü Aras, *Görüşlerim*, vol. 2 (Istanbul, 1968) pp. 229–30.
    On the other hand, the fact that Turkey wanted to obtain its rightful demands in the Straits through legal channels and not by creating *faits accomplis* or by using force aroused sympathy in Britain. For instance, in a memorandum on this question prepared by the British Foreign Ministry on 23 July 1936, it was stated that 'that [Turkey] suggested revision by negotiation was in happy contrast with certain other recent procedures . . .' FO 371/20080; E4702/26/44.
15. Sir G. Clerk's report from Ankara dated 31 December 1932; FO 371/16011; E6030/6030/65.
16. FO 371/16987; E6297/6294/44.
17. FO 371/17967; E4048/4048/44.
18. FO 371/17966; E4525/3652/44.
19. Turco-British relations in this period were not without frictions. For instance, in the summer and autumn of 1934, when some British warships in the Aegean were fired at by Turkish guards, Turkey did its best to settle the incident in a friendly way. (Mr Morgan's report from Istanbul dated 7 October 1934: FO 371/17969; E6224/4542/44.) On the other hand, in a speech at the House of Commons on 24 July 1934, Mr Drewe said that the eggs imported from Turkey were sold very cheap in Britain (about $\frac{1}{3}$ cheaper) and that the British producer could not compete with them (292 HC (House of Commons), Deb. 5s., pp. 1651–2). During the sitting on 14 November 1934, Captain Fuller asked what was the effect of the Turkish textile industry upon Britain: (293 HC Deb. 5s., p. 1974). Lieut.-Colonel Colville said the following on behalf of the Government: '. . . I am not able to estimate what effect the development of a Turkish textile industry is likely to have on the textile industries of this country'.
20. For further information see: Fahir H. Armaoğlu, *Siyasî Tarih, 1789–1960* (Ankara, 1973) p. 660.
21. Feridun Cemal Erkin, *Dışişlerinde 34 Yıl, Anılar-Yorumlar*, (Ankara, 1980) p. 83.
22. Idem.
23. FO 371/20094; E8015/5280/44.
24. FO 371/20861; E2258/315/44.

25. The relations with France, which had deteriorated due to the Sanjak question in the mid-1930s, rapidly improved from 1937 onwards – with indirect British encouragement. During a conversation held upon his request, the Turkish Ambassador to Britain Fethi Bey asked Mr Eden on 7 January 1937, whether Turkey could count upon Britain's good offices in the question of the Sanjak of Alexandretta. Eden replied that Fethi Bey could be sure that 'we would do anything we could to bring a settlement of this difficulty'. He added: 'We [are] very good friends both with Turkey and with France, so . . . it [is] in our interest . . . to do our utmost to bring about a solution'. (FO 371/20845; E149/3/89).

    Upon the conclusion of an agreement between France and Turkey, Sir Percy Loraine, in his despatch from Ankara dated 29 January 1937, said that the widespread opinion among Turks was that 'this result could not have been achieved without [Mr Eden's] personal happy and successful assistance', and that 'this development was interpreted as the strengthening of Turco-British friendship'. FO371/20846; E680/3/89.
26. The British Ambassador in Ankara, Sir Percy Loraine – who was a close friend of Atatürk – said in his 'Very Confidential' despatches to the Secretary of State dated 24 and 28 February 1937, that he had met Aras on 23 February; the latter told him that in the war looming ahead, 'Turkey would fight on the side of Britain'. (FO 371/20861; E1414/315/44.) In other words, Turkey, as early as in 1937, was determined to side with Britain.

    For the positive effect upon Turco-British relations of Sir Percy Loraine's closeness to Atatürk, see: Gordon Waterfield, *Professional Diplomat: Sir Percy Loraine of Kirkharle Bt. 1880–1961* (London, 1973) *passim*.
27. 352 HC Deb. 5s., pp. 1127–30.
28. Erkin, op. cit., pp. 136–8.
29. Ahmet Şükrü Esmer and Oral Sander, 'İkinci Dünya Savaşında Türk Dış Politikası', *Olaylarla Türk Dış Politikası (1919–1973)*, Genisletilmiş Üçüncü Baskı, (Ankara, 1974).
30. Ibid., pp. 194–195.

    Lord Kinross, during the interview referred to above, said that if Atatürk had been alive, he would have entered the War in early 1944 at the latest. 'The Balkans would not have fallen into the hands of the Soviet Union, and the outlook of the world would be different', he added.
31. Erkin, op. cit., p. 148.
32. Mehmet Gönlübol and Halûk Ülman, 'İkinci Dünya Savaşindan Sonra Türk Dış Politikası (1945–1965)', *Olaylarla Türk Dış Politikası (1919–1973)*, op. cit., pp. 219–22.
33. T.R. Aras (op. cit., p. 231), says that Turco-British relations should be analysed in two periods: Britain-Ottoman Empire and Britain-Turkey. The former 'started in friendliness; led to alliance and ended in

great animosity'. The latter, however, 'started in animosity and developed within NATO into the eternal alliance of today'.

34. On one occasion, Atatürk told a foreigner that the British were 'a nation of character'. Graves, op. cit., p. 227. In a 'Confidential' report dated 30 March, 1927 from Mr Hoare (Istanbul), it was reported that during a ball in Ankara, Gazi Mustafa Kemal 'made frequent flattering references to Great Britain'. He praised the British, saying that they were 'the greatest nation in the world; the world's greatest coloniser; . . . the people in whose fairness he trusted; the nation, which, by its valour and perseverance, had succeeded in building up the greatest of all empires'. FO 371/12308; E1575/17/44.
35. In a despatch dated 31 August, 1919, the British chargé d'affaires in Athens, Mr Russell, said that the personality of the Greek was not attractive but that the Turkish character strongly resembled the feelings of most of the British. Gotthard Jaeschke, *Kurtuluş Savaşı İle İngiliz Belgeleri* (Tr. Cemal Köprülü), (Ankara, 1971) p. 141.
36. Geoffrey Lewis (*Turkey*, 3rd ed., London, 1965) p. 206, mentions this similarity between the two nations and says that the Turks 'are the English of the East'.

VIII

ANGLO-TURKISH TRADE SINCE 1923: EXPERIENCES AND PROBLEMS

William Hale

In seeking to explain the evolution of trade between two countries one is faced with the task of trying to follow a single thread in an extremely complicated pattern. Whether a country buys goods from another, of what type and in what quantity, is not decided by a single general bargain. It is deeply affected by the competitive position of other suppliers, the rate and direction of economic development in each of the trading partners and by overall trends in the world economy. Much of this paper is not specifically about Anglo-Turkish trade, but a broader treatment is often necessary if one is to explain (rather than just narrate) the main theme. The story is divided into four sections, each of which covers a reasonably distinct period, though the last period (beginning in 1945) is treated much more briefly than its relative importance would probably warrant.

THE LIBERAL PHASE: 1923–29.

In the modern history of Turkey's foreign trade, the first six years of the Republic stand out as a liberal era. At this time, Turkey had an almost free trade regime, with a low import tariff and virtually no quantitative restriction of imports. Her currency was freely convertible and was, in effect, allowed to float on the international exchanges. Hence, Turkey's experiences during the 1920s offer an interesting test case of the effects of free market conditions on the international trade of a developing country.

The set of policies was not entirely a matter of free choice for the Turks: it was mainly the result of tariff restrictions contained in a Commercial Convention attached to the Treaty of Lausanne, which obliged Turkey to apply the Ottoman customs tariff of 1916, until 1929. This was a specific tariff fixing duties in Liras on different categories of imports, by volume. The Turkish Government was permitted to increase the duties in 1923, to allow for the decline in the value of the Lira since 1916, but this still left them at about the real levels of 1916.[1] Calculations by Çağlar Keyder show that the weighted average protection rate for Turkey's main imports in 1928 was 12.4%. This was a low tariff (especially by later standards) and meant that if infant industries were to be protected then they would have to be given non tariff incentives, like those contained in the Encouragement of Industries Law of 1927.[2] A natural side-effect of this restriction was that Turkey was unable to discriminate between one trading partner and another, so that foreign suppliers were left to compete with one another in the Turkish market on equal terms.

How did these conditions affect the overall development of Turkey's foreign trade in the 1920s? A precise answer is not easy to give, since the officially published statistics on imports and exports under-report both items.[3] Nevertheless, it appears that Turkey consistently ran an international trade deficit, amounting to about 10–15% of her total foreign trade. This caused serious concern to the Turkish authorities and pushed down the value of the Lira against most foreign currencies throughout the decade.

It is against this background that we can assess trends in Britain's trade with Turkey. At the outset, it has to be remembered that the British had played a dominating role in pre-war years, accounting for as much as 19% of Turkey's total imports.[4] They retained this dominance in the trade of Istanbul during 1919–21, when their political influence in the Sultan's capital was paramount and the former central powers (notably Germany) were excluded from the Turkish market.

After peace was restored, however, the British merchants' predominance was gradually eroded, as the figures in Table 1 indicate.[5]

Table 1: Anglo-Turkish Trade, 1924–29 ($m)

	1924	*1925*	*1926*	*1927*	*1928*	*1929*
Imports[(a)]	18.2	20.6	17.3	14.9	14.0	15.2
As % total imports	17.7	15.7	14.1	13.6	12.3	12.2
Exports[(b)]	12.3	9.4	11.2	8.7	9.0	7.1
As % total exports	14.6	8.9	11.4	10.6	10.1	9.6
Balance[(c)]	−5.9	−11.2	−6.1	−6.2	−5.0	−8.1

(a) Turkish imports from Britain. (b) Turkish exports to Britain. (c) Exports minus imports. Data converted from TL at current exchange rates, to allow for decline in international value of the Lira.

Source: *İstatistik Yıllığı 1932–33*, pp. 254–55.

Two points stand out in the pattern illustrated in Table 1. The first is that the balance of trade between the two countries was persistently in Britain's favour. This was not purely a reflection of Turkey's overall trade deficit, since the imbalance in trade with Britain was greater, proportionately, than that of her total foreign trade. In a free trade system, such as then applied, this was not a fatal defect, since Turkey was able to make up part of her deficit with Britain by running a regular surplus in her trade with the United States, Italy and Greece.[6] Nevertheless, it certainly played an important part in the generation of the overall deficit.

Another striking trend is the almost continuous shrinkage of Britain's trade with Turkey, both absolutely and proportionately. In 1924 Britain supplied almost 18% of Turkey's imports and took between 14% and 15% of her exports. By 1929 these proportions had fallen to 12% and 10% respectively. The British Commercial Attaché in Istanbul, C.H. Courthope Munroe, recognised the beginnings of this decline as early as 1922, and his diagnosis was to become a familiar one. British firms, he complained, tended to assume that their inherited reputation for quality would continue to bring a stream of customers to their doors; they failed to advertise their goods properly or adopt the aggressive marketing tactics of their competitors.[7]

These criticisms were probably well founded; it has to be added, however, that not all the decline can be explained by the British traders' sluggishness. It seems likely that another important factor was that cotton textiles were by far the most important of Britain's exports to Turkey, and that this was precisely the industry in which natural endowments allowed Turkish firms to expand their own output, in spite of the low import tariff. To take the reasonably typical year of 1926, cotton textiles and yarn accounted for over 55% of Turkey's imports from Britain (Table 2). On the other hand, the share of textiles in Turkey's total import bill fell during the decade, just as that of metals and machinery needed for the new factories tended to increase (Table 3). In effect, the switch to imported textiles, especially from Britain, which had gathered pace during the nineteenth century, was now beginning to reverse.

The story needs further explanation, however, since it will be noticed that in absolute, rather than proportionate terms, Turkish textile imports grew during the decade, whereas imports from Britain dropped absolutely. Britain's decision to move back to the gold standard in 1925 at the pre-war parity may account for this. Between 1924 and 1929 the average value of sterling on the Istanbul exchange moved upwards against the Lira by about 23%. During the same period, the dollar exchange rate increased by only 10%, while that of the French franc actually fell by 20%.[8] The conclusion is that British traders may well have found themselves priced out of the Turkish market by rivals from countries with more competitively valued currencies.[9]

The decline in Turkey's exports to Britain is far more difficult to explain. A striking feature is that tobacco represented only a tiny proportion of British imports from Turkey, although this was easily Turkey's most important export.[10] The share of tobacco in total exports fluctuated during the decade, so it is hard to link the decline to the atypical compo-

Table 2: Structure of Anglo-Turkish Trade, 1926

Turkey's Imports from Britain			Britain's Imports from Turkey		
Commodity	*Value (TL m)*	%	*Commodity*	*Value (TL m)*	%
Wool textiles	4.6	13.9	Tobacco	0.2	0.9
Cotton textiles & yarn	18.3	55.5	Fruit & nuts	8.2	38.5
			Mohair	4.3	20.2
Other	10.1	30.6	Other	8.6	40.4
Total	33.0	100.0	Total	21.3	100.0

Source: *İstatistik Yıllığı 1932–33*, pp. 255, 268–86, 289–301.

Table 3: Structure of Turkey's Imports, 1923–28

Commodity	*1923*		*1926*		*1928*	
	$m	%	*$m*	%	*$m*	%
Cereals & flour	8.7	10.1	3.3	2.6	8.7	3.9
Sugar, etc.[(a)]	9.0	10.4	10.6	8.6	20.4	9.1
Textiles	37.4	43.4	48.8	39.6	68.2	30.5
Metals & machinery[(b)]	5.8	6.7	20.4	16.6	44.9	20.1
Other	25.4	29.4	40.2	32.7	81.3	36.4
Total	86.3	100.0	123.4	100.0	223.5	100.0

(a) Includes 'colonial products' (coffee, tea, etc.). (b) Includes vehicles.

Source: *İstatistik Yıllığı 1932–33*, pp.257–8. Data converted from TL at current exchange rates.

sition of Turkish exports to Britain. A possible explanation is that the total market for Turkey's export goods was growing faster in other countries than in the UK, but a full exploration of this possibility lies outside the scope of this brief survey.

THE CONTROLLED PHASE: 1930–39.

The beginning of the 1930s marked a watershed in both internal and external trends in the Turkish economy. With the onset of the world depression, there was a general collapse of confidence in the free market system. This combined with the somewhat disappointing experience of liberalism in the 1920s to reorient Turkish economic policies. Turkey's development did not and could not become entirely autarchic, but the adoption of etatism as official policy meant a greater emphasis on industrial planning and state-run industry at home, and a protective and controlled foreign trade regime.

The first change came in 1929, with the expiry of the tariff restrictions of the Lausanne Treaty. Import duties were immediately raised, especially on consumer goods. During the following two years strict foreign exchange and import controls were introduced.[11] As from September 1931, import quotas on a wide range of goods were applied.[12] These controls were reinforced by a series of bilateral trading agreements with most of Turkey's main trade partners. Under these arrangements, Turkey's imports from any one country were generally restricted by the value of its exports to it, and vice versa.[13] These agreements ended the persistent deficit in the balance of trade which Turkey had previously experienced, but they also biased imports in favour of those countries which bought most from Turkey.

As a result of these measures, Turkey's foreign trade showed a positive balance for every year between 1930 and 1939 but for 1938, when imports surged upwards, to complete the first five year industrialisation plan (1934–38). Adding imports and exports together, total foreign trade dropped from $141 million in 1930 to $89 million in 1932, at the trough of the world depression, but then recovered to $234 million by 1938.[14] These swings were accentuated by a fairly sharp fall in prices during the early thirties and some rise thereafter, but nevertheless indicated the extent to which Turkey's foreign trade was influenced by world conditions, as well as the new trade regime.

Britain was slower than some of Turkey's other trading partners to negotiate a bilateral clearing agreement. The Anglo-Turkish Treaty of Commerce and Navigation of 1930 gave reciprocal most-favoured-nation treatment but did not contain provisions to balance the trade between the two countries. Since Turkey's imports from Britain were still higher than Britain's imports from Turkey the Treaty was denounced by the Turkish Government in 1935. In September of that year it was succeeded by a new Trade and Payments

Agreement, which was supplemented by a Clearing Office Order introduced in 1936. By a system of blocked accounts, this aimed to restrict Turkey's imports from Britain to the level of her exports to the UK. Unfortunately, this failed to redress the balance, which remained in Britain's favour for all but two years (1936 and 1937). The result was that British exporters were left waiting for months, or even years, on end for settlement of their accounts in sterling.[15] In 1938 the two Governments agreed to the crude step of restricting Turkey's annual imports from Britain to £500,000, but this seems to have been quite ineffective.[16]

The British authorities also granted Turkey important lines of credit. The first, of £3 million, was made available in 1936 by the British Export Credit Guarantee Department (ECGD) for equipment for the Karabük iron and steel works, which was being supplied by the British firm of H.A. Brassert. The ECGD followed this up in 1938 with a further £10 million credit for the import of British goods ordered before the end of 1940. Finally, Turkey received a special armaments credit from Britain, worth £6 million, in 1938.[17] Apart from the need to help their exporters, the British were almost certainly inspired by the political objective of winning Turkey over to the British side in the looming war with Germany. However, these initiatives were of no benefit to British firms whose exports were not covered by the credit agreements. In March 1939, for instance, the delay in payments from Turkey still stood at around twenty-seven months.[18]

The problems which underlay this story are illustrated in Table 4, which shows aggregate figures for Anglo-Turkish trade during the thirties. Apart from the imbalance, which naturally worried the authorities, there was also a fairly persistent fall in Britain's share of Turkey's overseas trade – in effect, a continuation of the trend of the 1920s. Part of this may be explained by factors noticed earlier – in particular, the take-over of the domestic textiles market by Turkish mills. Above all, the system of bilateral clearing agreements severely restricted Anglo-Turkish trade. Understandably, British firms were reluctant to sell to Turkey if they knew they would be faced with long delays in payment. These occurred because the Turkish Central Bank was permanently short of sterling – in other words, because of the shortage of Turkish exports to Britain. Turkey's clearing agreements with Germany were largely responsible for this. A totalitarian state like the Third Reich could afford to ignore the world market when fixing import and export prices. Accordingly, Turkish exporters were offered artificially high prices in Germany. Turkey could not use the proceeds to pay for imports from other countries, like Britain, since the Reichsmark was non-convertible. Germany also made up for the potential loss to herself by charging artificially high prices for her exports. It was quite understandable that a Turkish firm exporting, say, raisins, would be unwilling to sell to Britain unless it had already sold all it could to Germany – and Germany was usually willing to buy all the goods on offer. The result is illustrated in Table 5. Germany supplied over half of Turkey's total imports in 1939 and took almost one third of her exports. Britain was not the only loser from this, since the increase in Germany's trade was greater than Britain's loss. However, this pattern illustrates the severe distortion which the bilateral agreements caused.

THE WAR PERIOD: 1939–45.

The outbreak of the Second World War had crucial effects on Turkey's foreign trade. Fluctuations in her political relations with the Allies and the Axis powers created violent swings in the direction of imports and exports. The prices of the primary commodities which Turkey exported were meanwhile driven upwards by competitive buying by the two warring sides. On

Table 4 Anglo-Turkish Trade, 1930–39, TLm.

	1930	*1931*	*1932*	*1933*	*1934*	*1935*	*1936*	*1937*	*1938*	*1939*
Imports[(a)]	16.5	14.4	10.6	10.1	8.6	8.7	6.1	7.1	16.8	7.4
As % of total	11.2	11.4	12.3	13.5	9.9	9.8	6.6	6.2	11.2	6.2
Exports[(b)]	13.5	10.8	10.0	8.6	5.3	5.2	6.4	9.8	4.9	7.3
As % of total	8.9	8.5	9.9	8.9	5.7	5.4	5.4	7.1	3.4	5.7
Balance[(c)]	−3.0	−3.6	−0.6	−1.5	−3.3	−3.5	+0.3	+2.7	−11.9	−0.1

Sources: *İstatistik Yıllığı 1936–7*, pp. 223–4; *İstatistik Yıllığı 1942–5*, p. 350.

Table 5 Turkey's Trade with Germany and Britain 1930–39

	1930	*1933*	*1936*	*1939*
Imports (TL m.)				
From Germany	27.4	19.0	41.7	60.1
As % of Total	18.6	25.5	45.1	50.9
From Britain	16.5	10.1	6.1	7.4
As % of Total	11.2	13.5	6.6	6.2
Exports (TL m.)				
To Germany	19.8	18.2	60.0	47.5
As % of Total	13.1	18.9	51.0	31.3
To Britain	13.5	8.6	6.4	7.3
As % of Total	8.9	8.9	5.4	5.7

Sources: As for Table 4.

Table 6 Turkey's Trade Balance, 1939–45 (TLm)

	1939	*1940*	*1941*	*1942*	*1943*	*1944*	*1945*
Imports	118	69	74	147	203	164	126
Exports	127	111	123	165	257	232	218
Balance	+9	+42	+49	+18	+54	+68	+92

Source: *İstatistik Yıllığı 1942–45*, p. 347.

Table 7 Turkey's Exports and Imports by value and volume, 1939–45

	1939	*1940*	*1941*	*1942*	*1943*	*1944*	*1945*
(1) Value, TLm	127	111	123	165	257	232	218
(2) Index (1939 = 100)	100	87	97	130	202	183	172
(3) Volume, 000 tonnes	1,1341	658	428	335	333	345	309
(4) Index (1939 = 100)	100	58	38	30	29	30	27
(5) (2) ÷ (3) × 100	100	150	255	433	697	610	641
(6) Imports by volume[a]	100	49	42	47	53	45	47

[a] Index: 1939 = 100

Source: As for Table 6

the other hand, the industrialised countries were concentrating their productive resources on the war effort and had little left over for export to neutral countries like Turkey. This meant an involuntary restriction of Turkey's imports. The result was that she ran a trade surplus (and in most cases a substantial one) for all the wartime years (see Table 6). By the end of the war, gold and hard currency reserves had been built up to a peak of $262 million.

The increase in export earnings during the war was due to a rise in prices rather than volume. This point is illustrated in Table 7. By 1943 the value of exports was more than double that of 1939, though it fell slightly during the last two years of the war. On the other hand, the volume of exports in 1945 was little more than a quarter of what it had been in 1939, implying that export prices increased by some six or seven-fold during the war.[19] Import prices also rose, but the signs are that the increase was less steep than for exports.[20] Evidently, Turkey gained from improving terms of trade.

The war years also saw a substantial recovery in Anglo-Turkish trade, both in absolute terms and as a proportion of Turkey's total imports and exports. Throughout the war, the direction of trade was heavily influenced by potential alliances and conflicts. During 1940–41, trade with Germany was cut back sharply. The Turks were understandably worried by the Nazi-Soviet Pact of August 1939 and shortly thereafter, on 19 October, signed a Treaty of Mutual Assistance with France and Britain. In a separate agreement, the British and French pledged a £23 million armaments credit, a gold loan of £15 million and a credit of £31 million for commercial goods.[21] During 1941, however, İnönü's Government became somewhat less wary of an attack by Hitler. In March of that year, when occupying Bulgaria, the Führer assured the Turkish President that German forces would not come to within 60 km of the frontier with Turkey. On 22 June the Nazis launched their long-planned attack on Russia. The invasion must have provoked a heart-felt sigh of relief in Ankara, since it eliminated the danger of a combined Nazi-Soviet attack on the Straits. Four days before, Turkey had signed a non-aggression pact with Germany. In July 1940 a commercial agreement with the Third Reich had been negotiated; this was followed in October 1941 by a second trade accord referred to as the 'Clodius agreement', after its chief German negotiator. As the figures in Table 8 show, trade with Germany recovered rapidly after 1941, to reach a peak in 1943. By 1944, however, the eventual allied victory was becoming more certain. In April of that year, Turkey finally ceased all deliveries of chromite to Germany, before severing diplomatic ties with the Reich on 2 August. By 1945, Turco-German trade was at a standstill, and the United States had replaced Germany as Britain's main commercial competitor in Turkey.[22]

Table 8 Turkey's Trade with Germany and Britain 1939–45

	1939	*1940*	*1941*	*1942*	*1943*	*1944*	*1945*
Imports (TLm)							
From Germany	60.1	8.1	8.9	41.0	76.6	50.2	0.8
As % of total	50.9	11.7	11.9	27.8	37.7	30.4	0.6
From Britain	7.4	9.7	18.4	34.7	32.3	29.5	29.5
As % of total	6.2	14.0	24.6	23.5	15.9	17.9	23.3
Exports (TLm)							
To Germany	47.5	9.7	26.9	40.8	61.1	52.9	—
As % of total	31.3	8.7	21.8	24.7	23.8	78.2	—
To Britain	7.3	11.5	20.0	25.2	27.9	51.4	32.6
As % of total	5.7	10.4	16.2	25.3	10.8	76.0	14.9

Source: *İstatistik Yıllığı 1942–45*, pp. 349–50.

The importance of chromite in Turkey's wartime trade derived from the fact it is an essential ingredient in steel-making and that Turkey accounted for almost 20% of the world's output in 1939. If the Allies could have denied the Germans access to this vital mineral they would have dealt a serious blow to the Nazi war effort. In October 1939 the Turkish Government proposed to the British to sell them 200,000 tonnes of chromite for the next two years. Since this was greater than Turkey's total output in 1939, such a deal would have pre-empted Germany from the market. Ankara then added that the British should also promise to buy specified quantities of perishable farm products, such as nuts, raisins and tobacco, on the grounds that Germany would probably refuse to continue purchasing these crops if she were prevented from buying chromite. In December 1939 Numan Menemencioğlu, who was then the Secretary-General of the Turkish Foreign Ministry[23] even offered to extend the chromite deal with Britain to twenty years. Later on, the British were to regret bitterly that they turned this offer down. In the event, they only promised to buy 50,000 tonnes of chromite per year in 1941 and 1942, with an option on that mined in 1943. They actually purchased considerably more chromite than the minimum promised (over 100,000 tonnes, for instance, in 1941) besides large quantities of agricultural products. To carry out their pre-emptive purchasing plan, they established a United Kingdom Commercial Corporation early in 1940: this was followed by an American equivalent, the USCC in 1942.[24]

The failure of the British to accept Menemencioğlu's offer of a long-term deal left Turkey free to recommence chromite sales to Germany. Under the Clodius agreement, about 47,000 tonnes were shipped during 1943. The continuation of chromite shipments to Germany in the early part of 1944 caused some bitter complaints by the British and Americans. The US Ambassador in Ankara, Laurence Steinhardt, even suggested that the Allies should take 'appropriate steps' to destroy the bridge across the river Maritza, which the chromite trains crossed on their journey to Germany, and was told by Menemencioğlu that he was surprised that this had not already been done.[25] In fact, it appears that Turkish deliveries to Germany were more restricted by Germany's limited ability to send manufactured goods in return than by the Allies' pre-emptive purchasing programme. The Turks stuck strictly to the letter of their agreements with both sides. Although the war brought some serious dislocations to the Turkish economy (in particular, rampant inflation and a serious shortage of imported goods) Inönü's Government succeeded in walking a delicate diplomatic and commercial tightrope and left post-war Turkey with the benefits of a large wartime trade surplus.

GROWTH AND TRANSFORMATION: 1945–82.

With the opening of the post-war period, the Turkish economy entered a phase of sustained growth and structural change, which was also beset by some serious problems, political and social as well as economic. The Turkish economy was revolutionised, as Turkey moved into the ranks of the newly-industrialised countries. For the historian, however, the story of Anglo-Turkish trade becomes ever more difficult to disentangle from the overall development of Turkey's external economic relations. As world commerce shifted into a pattern of economic blocs, rather than individual nation-actors, so the evolution of Anglo-Turkish trade became a relatively small part of Turkey's relations with the EEC or with the industrialised world as a whole, rather than a separate bilateral issue.

Two important features of Turkey's foreign trade since the Second World War are illustrated by the summary statistics in Table 9. The first is that, even allowing for the declining purchasing power of the dollar, total foreign trade has increased impressively over the last twenty-five years, in line with the growth of the domestic economy. The second is that Turkey has consistently run a foreign trade deficit (in contrast to the pre-war period) and that this has led to regular and acute balance of payments crises – in particular, in 1957–8, 1968–9 and 1975–80. Of these, the last was nearly disastrous. The oil price rises of 1973–4 and stagflation in the western economies had a devastating effect on Turkey's external accounts. Weak governments failed to maintain a realistic exchange rate in the face of galloping inflation, so that exports stagnated while the costs of imports skyrocketed. By the late 1970s the deficit on current account had risen to between 40% and 50% of the

Table 9 Turkey, Balance of Payments, Current Account, 1946–82 ($m, annual averages)

	1946–50	*1951–60*	*1961–70*	*1971–5*	*1976–80*	*1981*
Imports	−245	−452	−684	−2,667	−5,156	−8,933
Exports	229	329	460	1,162	2,075	4,703
Net Invisibles	n.a.	−6	+44	+1,056	+844	2,138
Balance	−16[(a)]	−129	−180	−449	−2,237	−2,092
Deficit as % imports	6.4	28.5	26.3	16.8	43.4	23.4

[(a)] Merchandise trade only.

Sources: Hale, *op. cit.*, p. 230: *Briefing*, 6 Dec. 1982, p. 22.

value of imports. It was only in 1980 that this problem was seriously tackled. Regular adjustments of the exchange rate and additional incentives to exporters produced an encouraging increase in exports during 1981–2, which augured well for the more balanced and stable growth of foreign trade during the 1980s.

Besides these recurrent crises, structural changes in Turkey's foreign trade are also worth noting, since they had important effects on Anglo-Turkish commerce. As Table 10 indicates, the share of investment goods in total imports tended to move upwards between the early 1960s and the mid-seventies, while that of consumer goods fell almost to vanishing point. This was a predictable result of the industrialisation of Turkey and the strict control of imports. On the other hand, the oil price explosion and the Turkish economy's growing oil dependence led to a rapid rise in the value of raw materials imports, which accounted for almost three quarters of the total by 1979 and had a restrictive effect on the inflow of capital goods. On the exports side, there was an equally impressive change. Turkish firms were becoming more competitive in a widening range of labour intensive industries. In 1981, for the first time in Turkey's history, manufactured goods accounted for a bigger share of total exports than traditional agricultural products. The evolution of Anglo-Turkish trade, shown in Table 11, fits into this general pattern. Trade in both directions grew in value, with a persistent surplus in Britain's favour for all but the early fifties. The growth in absolute terms, however, masks the decline of trade with Britain as a percentage of Turkey's total foreign trade. This point is made in Table 12. In 1950, the British still supplied about 10% of Turkey's imports (a higher share than for most of the 1930s) and retained roughly this proportion until the mid-seventies. Sales to Britain accounted for a lower proportion of total Turkish exports, but this was a pattern which had persisted since the earliest days of the Republic.

A rapid decline set in after the oil price explosion, which dramatically reduced the share of all OECD countries, including Britain, in both imports and exports. On imports, the

Table 10 Turkey, Structure of Imports & Exports, 1963–81

	1963–7	*1968–72*	*1973–8*	*1979–81*
Total Imports				
($m., ann. ave.)	640	1,000	4,354	7,304
of which (%)				
Investment goods	34.7	31.6	39.6	24.6
Raw materials	54.9	58.0	56.9	73.3
Consumer goods	10.3	10.4	3.5	2.0
Total Exports				
($m., ann. ave.)	451	610	1,403	3,291
of which (%)				
Agricultural prod.	79.3	74.3	60.1	53.0
Minerals	4.0	5.9	5.6	5.2
Manufactured prod.	16.7	19.7	34.2	41.8

Sources: Hale, *op. cit.*, p. 232: *İstatistik Cep Yıllığı 1982*, p. 207.

Table 11 Trade Balance with Britain, 1950–81 ($m)

	1950	*1961*	*1973*	*1978*	*1981*
Imports from UK	−30	−67	−223	−205	−434
Exports to UK	37	30	91	113	147
Balance	+7	−37	−132	−92	−287

Sources: *İstatistik Yıllığı* for 1951, 1962, 1975, 1979: *İstatistik Cep Yıllığı*, 1982

Table 12 British Share of Total Imports & Exports, 1950–81

	1950	*1961*	*1973*	*1978*	*1981*
Total Imports ($m)	286	509	2,086	4,599	8,933
Imports from UK ($m)	30	67	223	205	434
As % of total	10.3	13.1	10.7	4.5	4.9
Imports from OECD ($m)	—	—	1,612	2,791	4,279
As % of total	—	—	77.3	60.6	47.9
Total Exports ($m)	263	347	1,317	2,288	4,702
Exports to UK ($m)	37	30	91	113	147
As % of total	14.0	11.7	6.9	4.9	3.1
Exports to OECD ($m)	—	—	969	1,506	2,263
As % of total	—	—	73.6	65.8	48.1

Sources: as for Tables 11.

effect was obvious; Turkey could not reduce the volume of oil imports without serious damage to her economy (which in fact occurred). In exports, also, there was a striking shift towards the oil-exporting countries of the Middle East, where markets for both basic foodstuffs and manufactured consumer goods were expanding fast, and where Turkey had a natural geographical advantage over other suppliers. In 1981, Middle Eastern countries took just over 40% of Turkey's total exports, compared to 48% for OECD members (or 32% for the EEC). Exports to the Middle East were also growing far faster than to the western industrialised countries. Britain's falling share of Turkey's foreign trade thus has to be set in the context of the massive movement of world economic power towards the OPEC states, and the declining share of all the OECD countries. In 1973, taking imports and exports together, West Germany was easily Turkey's most important trading partner, to be followed at some distance by Britain and then by the USA and Italy. By 1981, Iraq had taken over a clear lead, ahead of West Germany, Libya and the United States. Britain, meanwhile, had sunk from the second position in

Table 13 Structure of Anglo-Turkish Trade, 1950, 1980

	1950		*1980*
Imports from UK			
Total	$30m.		$317m.
of which (%)			
Textiles	6.0	Chemicals	10.2
Iron & steel	7.6	Iron & steel	5.7
Machinery	35.1	Machinery	27.4
Vehicles	14.2	Vehicles	13.7
Other	37.1	Other	43.0
Exports to UK			
Total	$37m.		$105m.
of which (%)			
Fruit & nuts	40.7	Fruit & nuts	32.9
Tobacco	20.7	Tobacco	2.9
Mohair	8.2	Cotton & products	32.3
Other	30.4	Borax & salts	9.4

Sources: as for Table 11.

1973 to tenth in 1981, just behind Saudi Arabia. The fact that the British share declined faster than that of the OECD countries as a whole reflected the sluggish growth of Turkish exports to Britain as well as the loss of competitive edge by British suppliers.[26]

Table 13 also shows that there have been some important changes in the structure of Anglo-Turkish trade over the last thirty years. In 1950, Britain's once dominant textile industry still retained a toe-hold in the Turkish market. By 1980 this had been almost entirely eliminated. Indeed, the flow of trade in textiles had now been reversed, as cotton goods (both yarn and cloth) now accounted for a substantial part of Turkey's exports to Britain. Competition from cheaper textiles imported from Turkey, as from other newly-industrialised countries, has become a constant source of complaint by British textile firms. Among British exports to Turkey, machinery and vehicles were still the largest items, in 1980 as in 1950, but chemicals have now risen to an important position in the list, in line with increased demand from Turkish industry. Nevertheless, trade in the opposite direction is still dominated by Turkey's traditional exports – fruits, nuts and minerals. In spite of the rise in Turkey's total industrial exports, only textiles seem to have made a significant impact on the British market.

SOME TENTATIVE CONCLUSIONS.

Clearly, the story will not end in 1983. In the future, trade between Britain and Turkey is likely to be affected by Turkey's possible accession to full membership of the EEC and Britain's possible withdrawal (especially if a future Labour Government carries out the Party's declared intentions on this score). The growing demand for protectionism, in Britain as in other industrialised states, threatens us with a stormy passage in commercial relations over the next few years. Looking back over the last six decades, however, certain tentative conclusions can be drawn.

Firstly, (and with the important exception of the wartime period) political relations seem to have had remarkably little influence on mutual trade. The wholesale switch from Britain to Germany as an industrial supplier during the 1930s did not reflect a political alliance with the Nazis – rather the reverse. Just before the war, political factors may have prompted the British to regenerate trade with Turkey, but this initiative does not seem to have had any clear effects until after the war had begun. Equally, during the post-war period, Turkey's membership of NATO and association with the EEC has not prevented the erosion of the shares of Britain and the other western industrialised states in Turkey's total foreign trade.

Secondly, long-run change in the Turkish economy has been the most important determinant of the structure of trade between the two countries. In 1923 Turkey had almost no industry. Almost all manufactured goods, including everyday consumer items, were imported and virtually all exports consisted of unprocessed primary products. By the 1980s, imported consumer goods have virtually disappeared from Turkish shops[27] and the rise of new industries has vastly broadened the range of exports. In effect, both sides have to climb up higher rungs of the technological ladder if trade is to be expanded.

Thirdly, the last ten years have witnessed a striking reorientation of Turkish trade towards the Middle East, which now rivals the EEC in importance, both as a market and as a supplier. This may prove to be no more than a passing trend (especially if oil prices fall in real terms). Nevertheless, it is a change which has some important implications for Turkey's future commercial relations with Britain and with the EEC as a whole.

NOTES

1. Some detail may be added to explain the background to this restriction. Before the First World War the Ottoman Empire had been bound by international treaties to apply a low *ad valorem* tariff, in which rates were raised from 7% to 11% in 1907. This was replaced by the specific tariff in 1916. After the war, the allied occupation forces in Istanbul forced the Sultan's Government to re-apply the pre-war tariff. Meanwhile, the National Government in Ankara continued to apply the 1916 tariff in the regions it controlled, increasing the duties five-fold.

Immediately after resuming control over the whole country, but before the Treaty of Lausanne was signed, Atatürk's Government raised the multiplier from five to twelve, thus applying a fully protective tariff (which, given a free hand, the Republic would probably have preferred from the beginning). The Lausanne settlement allowed a five-fold increase for most imports and thus represented a compromise between the original aims of each side. C.H. Courthope Munroe, *Report on the Economic and Commercial Conditions in Turkey, 1922* (London, Dept. of Overseas Trade, 1922) p. 17; Çağlar Keyder, 'The Definition of a Peripheral Economy: Turkey, 1923–1929' (Ph.D. thesis, University of California, Berkeley, 1977: pub. Ann Arbor, University Microfilms Inc., 1978) pp. 120–2.

2. Keyder, op. cit., p. 123. This was not universally the case, however: see *infra*, f.n. 11.
3. Ibid., pp. 124–8.
4. This figure is for 1913/14: in 1884/85 it had been 46%. Charles Issawi, *An Economic History of the Middle East and North Afria* (London, 1982) p. 38.
5. Contemporary British reports put total imports into Istanbul in 1919 at TL 9.7 million, of which Britain provided TL 2.7 million, or about 28%. In 1920 the proportion rose slightly to 29%. C.H. Courthope Munroe, *General Report of the Trade and Economic Conditions of Turkey, 1921* (London, Dept. of Overseas Trade, 1921) Appendix IV(a).
6. *İstatistik Yıllığı 1932–33*, p. 253: Keyder, op. cit., p. 136.
7. Munroe, *Report . . . 1922*, p. 6.
8. *İstatistik Yıllığı 1932–33*, pp. 330–31. Data calculated from average values for each year.
9. It is worth adding that during the same period the exchange rate of the Italian Lira moved upwards by 28%, while Italy's share of total imports dropped from 21% in 1924 to 12.5% in 1929 – a parallel experience to that of Britain. However, the picture is confused by the fact that many goods originally exported from central Europe were shipped via Trieste and counted by the Turkish customs as imports from Italy. Ibid., pp. 254–5, 331.
10. See Table 2. This is a continuing feature of Anglo-Turkish trade and is explained simply by the fact that British consumers prefer Virginia tobacco. Non-smokers will argue that since smoking is an irrational habit anyway there is no point in investigating why smokers prefer one sort of tobacco to another.
11. There were some exceptions; in particular, import duties on cement and flour were lowered in 1929, since Turkish firms in these industries had already been making high profits under the old tariff. Keyder, op. cit., pp. 123–4.
12. William Hale, *The Political and Economic Development of Modern Turkey* (London, 1981) pp. 72–3.
13. The only important exception was the United States, with whom

Turkey had enjoyed a positive trade balance even under the old free trade regime. In most agreements, Turkey was permitted to retain a fixed percentage of her earnings in one country to pay creditors in another. In the case of Britain and Holland, for instance, the percentage was fixed at 30%, in that of France at 35%, and so on. In the case of trade with Germany, Turkey was allowed to accumulate a surplus of 30%, but could only use it for the purchase of German goods. H. Woods, *Report on Economic and Commercial Conditions in Turkey, 1936* (London, Dept. of Overseas Trade, 1936) p. 3.

14. Hale, op. cit., p. 73.
15. S.R. Jordan, *Report on Economic and Commercial Conditions in Turkey, April 1939* (London, Dept of Overseas Trade, 1939) pp. 40–1.
16. See Table 4.
17. Jordan, op. cit., pp. 31–2.
18. *Turkey: Review of Commercial Conditions, June 1945* (London, Dept of Overseas Trade, 1945) p. 24.
19. This calculation is not an exact one, since it does not allow for possible changes in the composition of exports – such as might occur, for instance, through a switch from bulky, low-price goods to low-volume, high-price commodities.
20. See Table 7.
21. See Edward Weisband, *Turkish Foreign Policy, 1939–1945* (Princeton, 1973) pp. 65–6, fn 88.
22. Ibid., pp. 103–4, 258–9: A Suat Bilge, *et. al., Olaylarla Türk Dış Politikası (1919–1965)* (Ankara Üniversitesi, Siyasal Biliger Fakültesi Yayınları 1969) pp. 151–5, 166, 172, 196–8.
23. He served as Foreign Minister between 1942 and 1944.
24. Weisband, op. cit., pp. 101–15.
25. Ibid., pp. 257–61.
26. Calculated from *İstatistik Yıllığı 1975* and *İstatistik Cep Yıllığı 1982*, pp. 208–11.
27. Turkish readers will realise that this sentence was written before the Özal Government's liberalisation of imports in 1984.

IX

TURKS AND BRITONS OVER FOUR HUNDRED YEARS

Geoffrey Lewis

An account of four hundred years of any human activity presented in the form of a single paper cannot hope to be more than a scrap-book. Any reference is deliberately excluded to most of the well-known people who might well have been discussed. This, for example, will be the first and last mention of Lady Mary Montagu. By this no disrespect to her is intended, nor to Thomas Dallam, nor to any other of the famous English writers about Turkey whose works are well known. The intention of this paper is to acquaint readers with the less familiar figures, the less widely read witnesses to the way in which Britons saw Turks, and to offer some personal observations. For those who are not closely acquainted with the relevant literature, two books could be recommended, one in English, one in Turkish: Harold Bowen's delightful *British Contributions to Turkish Studies* (London, 1945) and Berna Moran's brilliant annotated bibliography of English publications of Turkish interest from 1482 to 1699, *Türklerle ilgili İngilizce Yayınlar Bibliyografyası* (Istanbul, 1964).

There is a splendid Turkish proverbial saying, one version of which runs: *Paşanın atı nallanırken, kurbağa ayağını uzattı*; while the Pasha's horse was being shod, the frog stuck his foot out. I mean that I would like to mention briefly one of *my* earliest contacts with a Turk, on my first visit, in 1950. He wanted to know, somewhat insistently, what my business was in Turkey. I told him that I had been studying the language for many years and now wanted to see something of the country and the people. That did not satisfy his curiosity. 'Have you no family connection with Turkey?' he asked. 'Did any of your family ever live in Turkey?' With the tactlessness of youth I replied, 'Well, my father-in-law was a machine-gunner at Gallipoli.' 'Really?' he cried. 'So was mine!' And he threw his arms round me. Then I knew that among such people I would always feel at home.

The pictures which Britons and Turks had of each other in the early part of the fifteenth century, before the establishment of diplomatic relations are easy to describe and, from our modern standpoint, infinitely depressing. For the Turks, England, with the rest of Christian Europe, was the home of those who not only denied the prophethood of Muhammad but denied also that God was One. Not content with believing in a Trinity, the Christians, whose churches were full of pictures and images, seemed no better than idolaters; they were both *müshrikîn* and *putperest*. In English eyes, the Ottoman Empire was to be feared for its irresistible military strength and execrated as the political embodiment of Islam, the religion which denied the divinity of Jesus. Such few Christians as may have known anything at all of Islamic beliefs, if they were aware of the veneration Muslims accorded to Jesus as a Prophet, would not have been thereby appeased. Never to have heard of Jesus could be excused; to know of his existence and to regard him as less than God was not excusable. The Christian attitude is perfectly summed up in a line of the early-twelfth-century *Song of Roland*: 'Paien unt tort e crestiens unt dreit' — 'Non-Christians are wrong and Christians are right.' And the Islamic view was the mirror image of that. On the Turkish side, however, the picture changed after the middle of the sixteenth century, when Protestant England had removed the images from its churches. In Turkish eyes the English had ceased to be idolaters and were enemies of those European powers who were still idolaters.

What brought about the change in the English picture of the Turks was the need to find new markets for English manufactures. English merchants came to Turkey and the long slow process began, of discarding the ancient prejudices that had been built on ignorance, aggravated by travellers' tales. It would be pleasant to be able to say that mutual suspicion and dislike ended as soon as Englishmen and Turks met, but of course it did not, as everyone knows who has read the late Akdes Nimet Kurat's *Türk-İngiliz Münasebetlerinin Başlangıcı ve Gelişmesi*. Kurat points out that Harborne's successor, Edward Barton, in his despatches to London, maintained a critical attitude towards the Turks which could by no stretch be called friendly. Yet Barton, according to Mustafa Selaniki Efendi's *History*, read and wrote correctly in Turkish and had no need of interpreters: '*lisan-ı türkide fasîh okur yazar, tercümana ihtiyacı yok*.' He was also popular among the Turks for his assiduity in attending on the ruler to whom he was accredited. It is well known that he accompanied Sultan Mehmet III on his Hungarian campaign in 1596 and that the Sultan wrote to Queen Elizabeth I to commend Barton for his services on that occasion. It is not so well known that he had previously accompanied Sultan Murad III on campaign and was with him when the fortress of Raab (Yanik Kalesi) was captured from the Austrians in September 1594. The story of this earlier adventure was told at the Court of King James I in 1607 by Mustafa Cavuş, who was at that time the Ottoman envoy in London (although there is some doubt about his official status). It may be that Barton felt that if he betrayed too much sympathy for the Turks in his despatches home the Queen might doubt his loyalty, or he may just have been doing his duty as a diplomat by practising the art of dissimulation. Kurat shows that stories were circulating in quarters unfriendly to England, to the effect that Barton had not been a mere interested observer of the Sultans' battles; that he had actually killed Christians himself. That may help to explain why he thought it necessary not to sound excessively pro-Turkish in his reports to London. One may even carry conjecture to the point of suggesting that one purpose he had in going on campaign with the two Sultans was to erase the memory of his offences against the peace of the first of them. For on 17 June 1594, Murad III had had occasion to address a *ferman* to the

Kadi of Galata, quoting a complaint from a resident of Tophane, a retired Kadi of Mecca:

> The Ambassador of England is living with his staff at Tophane, in the house of Arab Ahmed Pasha, but they are far from being good neighbours. They are constantly practising debauchery and lewdness and many debauchees visit them and behave in a lewd fashion and they bring harlots and for ever engage in foul and loathsome conduct. This house being on the shore, they conceal runaway slaves and help them to escape. At the times of prayer they play drums, fifes and clappers and they empty garbage over Muslim graves and perpetrate many such corrupt acts. Muslims have therefore left notes saying, 'Either evict the Ambassador or we shall set fire to the neighbourhood. Their turpitude and their transgressions are inordinate. It is in every respect more advantageous to the Muslims that they should be in Galata, in the houses where they have always been.' Therefore has my glorious imperial *ferman* been issued, that they reside in the houses where they formerly resided. I order that, on the arrival of this my command, illustrious in power, you enjoin on, and confirm to, the said Ambassador, in accordance with the intention thereof, that he quit the house in question and go to reside in Galata, in the house where he formerly resided, desisting from committing the transgressions described. You will allow the said Ambassador to make no kind of excuses or pretexts but will at once evict him from the said house.

Let us leave Edward Barton and the debatable topic of whether or not he is to be counted as a Turcophile. What is gratifying is the speed with which some Britons overcame centuries of uninformed prejudice, went to see Turkey for themselves and liked what they saw.

Sir Henry Blount (1602–82) travelled overland to Istanbul in 1634. He stayed in the city just five days, which he mostly spent looking at the devastation left by the great fire of the previous year. Of the region in general, he says in his *A Voyage into the Levant* (London, 1636):

> Moreover, those pàrts being now possesst by the *Turkes*, who are the only moderne people, great in action, and whose Empire hath so suddenly invaded the World, and fixt it selfe such firme founda-

> ations as no other ever did; I was of opinion, that he who would beholde these times in their greatest glory, could not finde a better scene than Turky.

In giving his reasons for travelling there, he makes it plain that he did not fall into the error of so many modern travellers, the error of supposing that five days' sojourn in a city makes one an authority on it:

> First, to observe the Religion, Manners, and policie of the *Turkes*, not perfectly, (which were a taske for an inhabitant rather than a passenger,) but so farre forth, as might satisfie this scruple, (to wit) whether to an unpartiall conceit, the *Turkish* way appears absolutely barbarous, as we are given to understand, or rather an other kinde of civilitie, different from ours, but no less pretending.

From Istanbul he sailed with the Turkish fleet to Egypt:

> The strangest thing I found among the Turkish Mariners, was their incredible civilitie. . . . if at any time I stood in their way, or encombred their ropes, they would call me with a *Janum*, or *Benum*, terms of most affection, and that with an encline, a voyce, and gesture so respective, as assured me, their other words (which I understood not) were of the same straine.

He had two experiences of Turkish justice and would eternally remember it as being 'honourable to strangers':

> First at *Saraih*, in *Bosnah* where I was forced to Justice by a *Christian*, whom I had sore wounded, for threatening to buy me for a slave; when the cause was declared by two *Turkes* my companions; the *Judge* not only freed me with *words*, and *gesture* very respective, but fined my adversary at fortie *Dollars*, and menaced him with death, if any mischiefe were plotted against me. . . . I grew so confident of the *Turkish* nature, as when *Lances*, or *Knives*, were often set against me, I doubted not my selfe, unless it were by a *Drunkard*, or a Souldier *voluntier*; for drinke makes the *fancy* of the one uncertaine, and the other going to merit *Paradise* by killing of *Christians* was no safe company for mee. . . .

His opinion of Turkish food is not as low as you might think; bear in mind that when he says 'these are the three ordinary dishes . . . they want not other', he doesn't mean that they don't want any other, but that they don't lack any other:

> Their *Diet* is very full, and grosse; they will refuse all dainties for a peece of fat *Mutton*; that they seeth with *Rice*, which is the most general food they use; they call that mixture *Pilawe*, over it they put *milke* made thicke; and sower [*i.e.* sour] called *Yugurt*, with *Pease, Rice*, and *Mutton* they make their Porrage Churbah: these are the three ordinary dishes of *Turky*; they want not other, as Luxury, or necessitie require . . . [The] Turkish disposition is generous, loving, and honest; so farre from falsefying his promise, as if he doe but lay his *hand* on his *breast*, *beard*, or *head*, as they use, or chiefly break *bread* with me, if I had an hundred lives, I durst venture them upon his word, especially if hee be a naturall Turke, no More, Arab, or Egyptian. . . .

His appreciation of the virtues of the Turkish character did not extend to their music, but we must not attach great importance to this, any more than he did, for he makes it clear that he knew nothing of music, whether Turkish or English:

> The *Musicke* of Turky is worth consideration; through all those vaste Dominions, there runnes one tune, and for ought I hard no more, nor can every man play that; yet scarce any but hath a *fiddle*, with two strings, and at Feasts, and other meetings, will confidently play upon it, but hee knowes not to what tune, nor can play the same twice over; this I'm sure of; for to make experiment, I have ventured to play at divers meetings, pretending the ayers of my countrey, to note whether they had skill or no, and tooke so well as they have often made me play againe; then I found their skill and mine alike, for I never understood the least touch of any instrument.

A year or two after Blount, there came to Turkey William Seaman (1606–80), the first Englishman to write a Turkish grammar, though he wrote it in Latin: *Grammatica Linguae Turcicae* (Oxford, 1670). He dedicated it to Lady Jane Merick, formerly the wife of Sir Peter Wych, the British Ambassador to Turkey from 1628 to 1639. He gave as a reason for dedicating it to this lady, of whom there is further mention below, 'because (during my youth) I began the study of the Turkish language while I was a servant of your family.' In the Preface to his grammar he explains his reasons for writing it:

> It is known to all how troublesome to all neighbouring nations and rightly feared by them has been the power of the Turks for many years back, nor can it be doubted that it would strike terror into other nations further removed if they were to win dominion over the Mediterranean Sea, which they largely surround. To which, now that the island of Crete has been lately [1669] subjugated, the road is open excessively wide, as if a bolt had been withdrawn (unless God bars the way). Not yet, however, are we sufficiently well acquainted with their affairs, their laws, customs, polity, their art of war and their literature, for it to be possible for the business of war and peace to be transacted with them conveniently and prudently, because their language, which is difficult enough and very rich, has hitherto remained unknown to Christians and neglected. Impelled by these considerations and principally by this concern, which is of the greatest moment, that the Christian faith and the truth of the Gospel be communicated to them in their vernacular tongue (For who knows whether or not God will grant them penitence whereby from them as from other nations He may select the people for His name?), and impelled in addition by the urging of eminent men, I have completed this Grammar and committed it to print. Indeed, to advance this same purpose I have ready a Turkish-Latin Lexicon, if subsidies be granted to print it.

In this we see the beginnings of a theme which constantly recurs: that it is the duty of the Christian to convert the Turk to Christianity. But in Seaman's words there is no trace of the ignorant contempt for non-Christians which too often characterises the writings of those who profess that duty. I am not saying that Seaman, who was an ordained priest of the Church of England, was not being patronising; it obviously *is* patronising to suggest that one's own religion is so manifestly superior to another man's that he has only to become acquainted with it to want to be converted to it. But Seaman at least accepts the Turks as reasonable fellow-men, and he does see the essential necessity to learn their language. In fact he made a translation into Turkish of the whole of the New Testament (Oxford, 1666), but it was not a very good translation and probably made few converts.

To return to the wife of Sir Peter Wych, there is a delightful story about her in a remarkable book by a Doctor of Medicine named John Bulwer, entitled *Anthropometamorphosis: Man Transform'd: or, The Artificial Changling* (London, 1653). The subject of the book is the devices employed by various peoples to change their natural appearance, by dress, by make-up or by actually deforming their bodies, for example by tattooing. I found several references in it to Turks.

> At this Day the *Grecians* and *Turks* have round heads much resembling a Globe, which they affect and nourish by Art in their Children, all holding it the most commodious forme to fit their Turbants and Shashes which they weare on their Heads.

His argument is not completely clear. He seems to be implying that Turks put turbans and sashes on their children's heads in order to make them into the round shape onto which one can most easily fit turbans and sashes; obviously a circular argument.

Next he talks about kohl, *göz sürmesi*:

> The *Turks* have a black powder of a Minerall called Alchole, with which they colour the Haire of their Eyebrows which they draw into embowed Arches. The Women affect very much black Eye-brows, and likely they are naturally so, if they be not, they die them into this hue by Art, made high and halfe Circular, and to meet if naturally they doe not.

Then comes a chapter entitled 'Our late great Verdingales'. The word may be more familiar in the form 'farthingales'', hooped petticoats, *çemberli iç etek*.

> Sir *Peter Wych* was Embassadour to the Grand *Signeour* from King James [that is a slip for 'King Charles I'], his Lady being then with him at *Constantinople*, the *Sultanesse* desired one day to see his Lady, whom she had heard much of; whereupon my Lady *Wych* (accompanied with her waiting-women, all neatly dressed in their great *Verdingals*, which was the Court Fashion then) attended her Highnesse. The Sultanesse entertained her respectfully, but withall wondering at her great and spacious Hips, she asked her whether all English woman were so made and shaped about those parts: To which my Lady *Wych* answered that they were made as other women were, withall shewing the fallacy of her apparell in the device of the Verdingall, untill which demonstration was made, the *Sultanesse* verily believed it had been her naturall and reall shape.

I have spoken of William Seaman. The next Englishman who tried to teach his countrymen Turkish was Thomas Vaughan. His *Turkish Grammar* deserves a brief mention. It was published in London in 1709. This is how he states his purpose in undertaking the task:

> I had no other View, than the Satisfaction and Advantage, which I supposed several Merchants abroad, and all who shall be design'd for Turky, might reap from such a Work. . . .
> And the Satisfaction of being able to return common Salutes, to set oneself in the right Road upon any little Excursions, and to reconcile ones self to the good Opinion of the Natives (had the Merchant no need of it in the Management of his Business) are sufficient inducements to the acquiring some Knowledge of the Language.

On the basis of certain internal evidence, Vaughan does not appear to have been a very attractive man. In view of that, as well as of the importance he attaches to winning the good opinion of the natives, his first Dialogue is particularly amusing; it seems to have been drawn from life. In it, the unfortunate English merchant is trying to write a letter but is not getting much help from his Turkish servant. And the servant appears to have a more highly developed sense of decent behaviour than the master:

Oteki gün iki akçelik mürekkep aldım idi; nice oldı? The other Day I bought two Aspers worth of Ink; what's become of it? *Nasıl öteki gün? İki ay geçti, belki dahi ziyade.* What other Day? 'Twas two Months ago, and perhaps longer. *Hâlâ getür bakayım.* Bring it now, I'll look. *İşte bak hem küflemiş, hem kurumuştur.* Look, see 'tis both mouldy and dry'd up. *Var imdi dükkândan bir akçelik al.* Go then, buy an Asper's worth at the Shop. *Vir imdi akçe.* Give me Money then. *Yanında bir akçe bulunmaz mı?* Have you not an Asper about you? *Kalmadı.* No. *Benimde ufak akçe yoktur.* I have no small Money. *Var viresi al, sonra virürüz; yoksa bize inanmaz mı dersin bir akçelik mürekkebe?* Go take it upon tick; we'll pay hereafter: or do you say he will not trust us for an Asper's worth of Ink? *İnanır, ama ayıptır.* He'll trust, but it's a Shame. *Var, çok söyleme.* Go, don't prate so much.

There are lengthy periods for which it has not been possible to find any items of special interest for this 'scrap-book'. One assumes that the Turkey merchants went on importing the sort of commodity which Thomas Vaughan lists in one of his dialogues: cloth, pig-lead, lead slabs, lead bars, red lead and white, tin, brass wire, pepper, ginger, steel, cochineal, watches, telescopes, spectacles and pistols, with divers other things. And some of the merchants doubtless behaved themselves and tried not to be nuisances to their Turkish neighbours, while others doubtless did not. There is a passage in Falih Rıfkı Atay's *Çankaya*, where he says that in the early part of our century Muslim Turks used to call Christians who were nice people *makul kefere*, 'reasonable unbelievers'; those not so nice, *gâvurlar* 'infidels'; but those who were really nasty pieces of work were *şapkalı gâvurlar* 'infidels with hats on'. Such distinctions must have existed in earlier centuries too.

As the Ottoman Empire ceased to be what Richard Knolles, writing in 1603, had called 'the present Terror of the World', it became possible for English people to see the Turks in a friendlier light. In 1786, just three years after the Montgolfier brothers' first balloon ascent, a Turk named Abdürrahman and a Persian physician constructed a balloon in which they took off from the gardens of the Saray in the presence of Sultan Abdülhamid I, and landed at Bursa. This feat seems to have escaped the attention of Turkish historians, but not of Turkey's English friends, for it was duly noted in Dodsley's *Annual Register of World Events*:

> We have before taken notice of the progress which arts and general knowledge are making in Constantinople, and that the grand signior had himself ordered the erection of printing-presses. . . . It was not, however, to be expected, that the new experiments and physical discoveries with respect to air, and the means of human conveyance through it, should have yet reached that capital . . . It was as little to be expected, that whenever such knowledge was communicated, or its effect displayed, the artist or adventurer should not have been a native of the Western world.

After a description of the ascent, the account goes on to contrast the enlightened attitude of the Sultan with that of the rulers of other nations:

> At the same time that this adventure excited so much pleasure, and was so amply rewarded at Constantinople, such is the difference of taste and opinion, that the proffered exertions of one of the most eminent aerial voyagers were rejected by the emperor of Germany, and the Prussian monarch; and all attempts of the kind were absolutely forbidden by the empress of Russia in any part of her dominions.

Information is the key to it all. Because some early journalist had taken the trouble to ascertain the facts about that balloon-ascent, to write the story and publish it, the English people who read that *Annual Register* began to form a higher opinion of the Turks than they had previously held. So did those individuals who took the trouble to visit Turkey. Among them was Lord Byron. This may be surprising; everyone knows that Byron spent his fortune and his life in winning for the Greeks independence from the Ottoman Empire – not an obvious candidate for the title of *Türk dostu*. But that same Byron wrote, in a letter to a friend in England:

> I see not much difference between ourselves and the Turks, save that they have long dresses, and we short, and that we talk much, and they little. . . . They are sensible people.

And this, in a letter to his mother:

> I have not been disappointed or disgusted. I have lived with the highest and the lowest. I have been for days in a Pacha's palace, and have passed many a night in a cowhouse, and I find the people inoffensive and kind. I have also passed some time with the principal Greeks in the Morea and Livadia, and, though inferior to the Turks, they are better than the Spaniards.

There never was a time in the last four hundred years when there were no English admirers of the Turks. The diplomatist David Urquhart (1805–77) went to Turkey in 1833 to look into the opportunities for British trade. When he came home he lectured on the merits of the Turkish bath, the *hamam*, and was responsible for building one in Jermyn Street in London. Writing of the insecurity of life in the last stages of the Byzantine Empire, he said its subjects must have been glad of 'the powerful protection of the Ottoman dominion, whose rule must have been indeed a happy change for the Greeks, when it was sought by the persecuted of Europe, and became the refuge of the Jews of Spain, and of the Protestants of Hungary.' A hundred and fifty years later, we can add to that 'and the Jewish and other victims of Nazi persecution.' For those interested in the continuity of history, let me add that Urquhart said:

> [Turkey's] position implicates [i.e., involves] its interest with those of all the great states of Europe, or at least four out of five. One has for its chief end, to create anarchy in Turkey.

It is not difficult to decide which one he meant.

Urquhart's contemporary, Adolphus Slade, the Sultan's naval adviser, was such a Turcophile that he did not approve of the Tanzimat reforms; he liked the Ottoman Empire just as it was. His writings are shrewd and entertaining. Here is a short passage from his comparison of the Istanbul prison, which he calls, 'the bagnio of Constantinople', with the prison-galleys of France:

> The galley slaves of Toulon, I positively assert, are one hundred times worse off than the inmates of the bagnio. The only point of resemblance is in their food, equally bad in each, consisting in a kind of hog-wash. . . . The galley slaves are chained in gangs – the bagniotes in pairs. The former must sleep on boards, the latter may sleep on beds. . . . The former have not the advantage of religion – within the precincts of the bagnio are a mosque, a Greek church, and a synagogue. In Toulon, there are four or five thousand galley slaves – in the bagnio the number rarely amounts to one hundred! for a city containing about half a million of souls, and the chief rogues of the empire.

Then there was Arthur Lumley Davids, a brilliant and tragic young man who died at the age of twenty-one, in 1832, having just completed his *A Grammar of the Turkish Language*. It is dedicated to Sultan Mahmud, 'by whose genius and talents the Ottoman Empire has been regenerated, and by whose institutions it has been raised to a distinguished rank among the kingdoms of Europe and Asia.' It is fair to say that, although as a grammar it is rather feeble, it is an attractive and readable book. Davids was far ahead of his time both in being devoted to the study of things Turkish and in deploring the way in which the virtues and achievements of the Turks were belittled by Europeans whose ignorance of them was almost total:

> Of all the people who have issued from Central Asia, the Turks are perhaps the most interesting. . . . Emerging from a primitive state of society, we view them passing through the various gradations which mark the progressive advancement of mankind, until arriving at the highest degree of civilization that the Asiatic race has ever attained. . . . [The] accomplished Osmanlis are making rapid strides towards rivalling the most learned and polished of the European States. . . .

One's conscience is not greatly troubled at omitting Elizabeth, Lady Craven, but one should not pass over Sir James Redhouse, author of the magnificent *Turkish-English Lexicon* (1890), of which Halide Hanım – Halide Edip Adivar – once said to this author, 'If it were not for that book, our beautiful old language would by now have been almost entirely lost to us.'

Equally, one cannot pass over E.J.W. Gibb (1857–1901), who loved Turkey but, so far as I know, never visited it; who died young but left as his abiding monument the six volumes of his *A History of Ottoman Poetry*. The great Persian scholar, Edward G. Browne, who saw it through the press, said in his preface, 'Whatever else may be alleged against the Ottoman Turks, it can never again be asserted by the candid and impartial reader that they are, or ever have been, indifferent to literature.'

It is not for everyone to aspire to being a Redhouse or a Gibb. We lesser mortals can only do our best to impart, at least to the English-speaking world, some knowledge of this great country and people, their language, history and culture. But often, alas, we feel we are butting our heads against a brick wall. More than twenty years after Atatürk presented his countrymen with the great gift of the new Turkish letters, a leader-writer in *The Times* of London, discussing the question of Turkey's entry into NATO, saw as an objection 'the fact that Turkey did not even use the Roman alphabet.' This man, whom I shall not do the honour of naming, subsequently wrote of this incident:

> Well, one should not make mistakes in *The Times* – or anywhere else for that matter – but the fuss! The Turkish Government sent for the British Ambassador and reprimanded him severely. The Foreign Office sent for the Foreign Editor and reprimanded *him* severely. And the Foreign Editor did his best to reprimand *me* severely (he was a very kind man). All this because of the absurd myth, which had not been true for many years, that *The Times* spoke for the British Foreign Office and always reflected British foreign policy.

But surely the answer to this light-hearted apologia is that there is no excuse for making a mistake of that magnitude when one is pontificating. Let us allow that particular journalist to fall back into well-earned obscurity, and say a word in praise of those journalists who do their utmost to present a fair picture of Turkey to the world. It would be invidious to mention their names, but tribute can at least be paid to one no longer with us, Patrick, Lord Kinross, who was proud to describe himself as a journalist and who wrote what is undubitably the best English biography of Atatürk. In that book there is an account of Anglo-Turkish relations on the very highest level: the friendship between Atatürk and King Edward VIII of England. And that reminds me of our present Queen's meeting, in 1971, with President Sunay. Those who witnessed the ceremony of welcome, or heard it on the radio, will always remember how the Queen, in her clear voice gave the traditional greeting, '*Merhaba asker*!', to the Guard of Honour at the airport, and how their reply, '*Sağ ol*!' rolled like thunder across the Anatolian plateau. Nor let us forget the diplomats, for, whatever was in Edward Barton's secret heart, modern British diplomats who have served in Turkey have all loved it, and all have done their share to foster the friendship of our two peoples; thus the President of the Anglo-Turkish Society is always a retired British Ambassador.

Of course, a government servant's overriding loyalty is to his own country, no matter how fond he is of another. In truth, that may hardly seem worth saying; but it is a means of introducing a story about Atatürk, for no lecture on any theme involving Turkey is complete without at least one. Falih Rıfkı tells of an evening at Atatürk's table:

> One night the Prime Minister brought a despatch from our Ambassador in London. I don't recall exactly what it was about, but the Head of State and the Prime Minister discussed it for a while at the table and decided how to answer it. Then they turned to face the rest of the company. At the far end of the table there was sitting Celâl Sahir, a rather dreamy poet, who raised his hand as if he were trying to catch the Speaker's eye in the Assembly. 'Were you going to say something?' said Atatürk. 'Please, let's

> hear it.' 'Sir,' replied the poet, 'as you have been discussing this problem openly in our presence, I take it we are entitled to state our views too. What I want to say is that the English, in their relations with other countries, are well-known for putting their own interests first.' 'Is that all you wanted to say?' asked Atatürk. 'Yes', said the poet. 'Then I thank you' said Atatürk, 'for your distinguished contribution to the discussion, both in my personal capacity and on behalf of the Government of the Republic.'

The Anglo-Turkish Society has been mentioned. Let me also refer to the Turco-British Association, which we know we can rely on to persuade any Turks who need persuading, that British people do not have two heads, even though some of us may be mistakenly supposed to have three Gods. In the last resort, we Britons and Turks must seek comfort in the words of one of the great poets of the world, Yunus Emre: 'What should the ignorant know of us? To those who know, our greeting' – '*Bilmeyen ne bilsin bizin? Bilenlere selâm olsun!*'

NAME INDEX